M000198924

Not Easily Washed Away

Memoirs Of A Muslim's Daughter

Anon Beauty

&

Brian Arthur Levene

GGP 2014
Chicago, IL

Not Easily Washed Away
Memoirs Of A Muslim's Daughter

Anon Beauty

&

Brian Arthur Levene

Gully Gods Publishing
www.gullygods.com

All rights reserved, including the right
to reproduce this book or portions
thereof in any form whatsoever

Copyright © 2014 Brian Arthur Levene
ISBN-10: 0983333009
ISBN-13: 978-0983333005

Why I Chose to Share My Story

As an adult who was sexually abused as a child, I decided I needed to stop focusing on myself so much and look at how I could help other people who have gone through — or are still suffering from — similar abuse. I wrote this book in order to do just that. When I met my fiancé, he thought the only way for me to heal from the abuse was to confront it fully. It worked. I became empowered, and my mind started to converge on the idea that I could have complete happiness and be accepted, even when people knew about my past. The story of my healing will show that there can be an end to the abuse and its physical, emotional, and psychological aftereffects.

Despite the fact that I knew my story would be difficult to write, I still wanted to share it so others could understand the manipulation that goes along with child sexual abuse. My goal was to show that such abuse affects a victim so traumatically that the perpetrator's manipulation can continue even after she reaches adulthood. One of the harder parts of confronting the abuse is the self-blame. Even though I thought I had let go of the abuse that happened years before, I still blamed myself and lived in shame and sadness for a long time afterward.

I realize that people from my traditional Muslim culture will find it hard to accept this book. Nevertheless, I wanted to show how my abuser used elements of that culture to perpetuate the abuse against me. My mother and others respected him as a hard-working Muslim man, one whose statements, he convinced me, would be believed in preference to those of a powerless young girl. It seemed like writing the story about what went through my mind as a child was the best way to convey how his manipulation worked.

I want people to understand that there is life after abuse and that victims should not let it ruin their whole lives. There is happiness after abuse. It is not easy, and by no means is anyone ever "cured" from child abuse, but one can live a normal life and free herself/himself from depression. Confront the abuse head-on, then forgive yourself and the abuser, and become strong so that you can live a happy life.

—Anon Beauty

Chapters

Anon Beauty & Brian Arthur Levene

Not Easily Washed Away

All names have been changed to protect the
interests of the parties mentioned in this book.

Chapter 1
The Second-Class Citizen

My sister Maya was born two years and eleven months after my birth. Both of us were born in Hyderabad, Pakistan, approximately a two hour drive from the main city of Karachi. After enduring a twenty-minute rickshaw ride through heavy Pakistani pedestrian traffic, my mother and Aunty Seema finally arrived at the broken-down maternity clinic. According to my mother, "the dingy hole-in-the-wall was not even fit for pigs to give birth in." The clinic had shoddy roofing, no hospital beds, and paint was stripping off the walls, showing the concrete blocks.

There was just a metal contraption draped by a white sheet with stirrups exposed for the birth of her newborn. "When your sister was out of her womb, and the midwife told her it was a girl, your mother started to bawl as if someone died." My mother's younger sister told me about the infamous day, laughing hysterically in our living room the first day of Ramadan in June 1991.

Confused about my aunt's remarks, I looked over to my sister to remind myself how pretty she was. She was born with big brown eyes, a beautiful face, and perfect olive skin, but she was deemed unacceptable for both our parents, and my father's family. My parent's first child, I was a daughter, not a son, and so I was no good to them as well. Yes: I am a daughter of Pakistan; therefore, in my society, I was born an unappreciated, second-class citizen. An unwelcome addition to my own family.

My mother, Ammi, was disdained, because her first child was not a boy. It wasn't her fault. After a year of living with my father's family, and being told what they expected from her womb, it was hard to accept anything else. She looked after me sparingly, most of her time spent being a slave to my father's family; the rest of her existence a torturous mix of sadness and depression.

My mother regretted marrying my father, entering into his family with their shamelessness. It was only a few days after their wedding day when her brother-in-law, Asim, tried to rape her.

When my mother told my father about his brother sitting on their bed, trying to touch her thighs and privates, porn playing in the background, my father pretended not to hear her. She knew my father and his family were beneath the ground she walked on, but she had to respect them out of wifely duty, spending her precious time slaving for them. When was she to love me? Her husband was gone most of the time to Saudi Arabia, where he worked, and when he was not there, she was left to bear the wrath of his family alone.

For the first two years of marriage my father and his family forbade my mother to see her family. My mother's family consisted of women who were educated with strong opinions about the way things should be in Pakistan. These opinions did not sit well with my father and his family.

At the time, most of the members of my father's family didn't even have high school diplomas. They felt threatened by my mother's family: so to control her, they isolated her from them, making her feel inadequate for not having a son.

If only I had been a boy she would have been treated better; if not by much, enough to make her think I was important. She described how unhappy and lonely she was after months of solitude and deprivation of love.

Her first pregnancy was extremely hard, and she was left to face her fears with no one to support or comfort her; no one to tell her about what to expect.

After I was born, she would put me down into bed, and weep for hours, crying out, "Allah, why have you betrayed me?" Her weeping was the predecessor for my lifetime of tears. I would ask Allah, "Why have you betrayed me?", and, "Allah, please take my life away!"

Although neglected most of our early childhood, my sister and I became well-adjusted, happy girls, making creative toys out of anything we could get our hands on. Our first source of fun was the water flowing from a tap standing in the middle of the floor of a roofless room on top of the house. The room had an orange concrete floor, and was surrounded by walls painted royal blue. It was once used to hand-wash soiled clothes in. Instead, we used it as our waterfall on hot, summer days. We became excited when rainbows formed in the puddles that formed in the middle of the room as the sun hit the pools of water.

When it rained in Pakistan we became elated, because it was time to play in the huge puddles of muddy water that rose up to our knees on the side of the road, soiling our dresses with muck that was not

so easily washed away. We con
my mother came out, and chas
how hard it was to wash the stair
with her bare hands. We would
pass the time while it rained, M
together for hours, listening to In
room broadcasting on the radio given to us by our
Aunty Salma, from Michigan. When our mother saw
us, she made fun of me, saying, "Fat people
shouldn't dance." I would quickly relinquish my
sister's hands, self-conscious about my appearance,
unable to continue my joy.

Chapter 2
"The Chicken Coop"

The house we lived in was modest, to say the least. It was in the heart of Karachi among the slums and the middle-class homes. My mother moved there the day she married my father. She had never seen the house before that day.

"If my mother knew he was bringing me to hell, she would have given me a pitchfork, to dance with Satan," she'd say in her less discreet moments, referring to her mother's lack of knowledge about her in-laws.

My grandmother had five daughters to marry off. Traveling the two hours from Hyderabad to Karachi several times to meet with my father's family, she did her best to make sure my father, Abdulla, was a good man. My grandmother told me how she stood at the bus stop in her burqa in order to see them, sweating so profusely people thought she had urinated on herself.

The house belonged to my father's father, who built it, but lived in his new home in the capital of Pakistan, Islamabad. My father had three sisters; two of whom were married off before my mother moved in. They lived in the house with his oldest brother, his wife, and their three children, which consisted of three regular-sized rooms built one on top of the other, the bathrooms built underneath the steps for each floor. The kitchen stood on the side of the house on the first-floor, behind the bathroom. The house was so small people would walk by, and say, "Looks like they're living in the chicken coop."

Outside of the house was a little porch made of green and brown, square, marble tiles. Everything except the walls was made of marble. Even the rolling pin to flatten dough for *roti* bread was made of marble. Decorative pieces, such as lizards, crocodiles, elephants, swans, chessboards, soap holders, and toothbrush holders, were all made from marble.

Using marble for everything was not by choice. The items were the defective pieces which could not be sold in my grandfather's marble showroom. There was no furniture on the first floor, which was used as the living room and the dining room. For comfort, four homemade cushions of green and red cloth were stuffed with old pieces of clothes and sewn together, then placed on the bare floor. The only other item in the living room was a nineteen-inch television that sat against the back of the room, across from the doorway entrance.

My father's older brother, Zafar, was a very eclectic individual. His second-floor apartment had a twin bed and a green metal wardrobe in it, big enough to fit my sister and I, and his son, who was eight at the time. We called it "the rainbow room" to lighten our spirits since the ceiling was red, the ceiling fan green, and the floor littered with yellow tiles, and black borders as trim.

The third floor was where my family lived. The room was split in half by an unpainted concrete wall with a wooden door in the middle of it. One side of the room was covered by two sheets of thick drywall that served as a divider to our small bedroom; the other, the uncovered laundry area where we played. That was the section that had steps leading downstairs.

My grandfather was middle-class, with a thriving marble business. His grand idea of creating a unique house was to replace the concrete flooring with square, yellow marble tiles. I used to imagine the black-colored borders were mountain trails, and the yellow was a swamp filled with alligators and crocodiles. I walked carefully on the borders, as to not let my feet touch the yellow tiles it surrounded. My mother passionately detested that house for many reasons, but her main tiff was the mismatched colors that, according to her, made the house look like a place "where circus clowns live."

My mother was an educated Muslim who finished high school, and was on her way to get her degree as a teacher. Because she was an educated woman, she paid dearly at the hands of her captors; her repression more tragic. My father's family was not educated, but still thought highly of themselves, considered them to be above my mother. She suffered the brunt of their ignorant elitism, and suffered severe punishment when they felt she was being "too smart for her own good."

My mother was a beautiful woman, with a smooth, round face, that gave the impression of kindness. Her full, luscious lips, and curly, long black hair, off-set that kindness with undeniable sensuality. If anything, this only enraged her in-laws. My mother was the bride of an arranged marriage, and according to Islamic law, obligated to treat her groom, and his family, like gods.

Day and night she slaved like Cinderella; but no fairy godmother came to her rescue. My mother was kind and loving to us on those moments she was happy, which were few and far between, yet stern, careless, and callous times when she was not.

Growing up I routinely saw both sides of my mother's personality, but before I was eight years old, mostly encountered the bad side. As children, both my sister and I were treated poorly. My sister was slightly luckier than I, due to her ailment. This affliction caused my mother to give her more attention than she gave me. I can't deny this made me resentful. Maya had jaundice from liver problems, and hardly ever ate.

When Maya would become ill, mother spent time nursing her back to health, feeding her, and making sure she took her medication. I remember wishing for a disease like my sister's so my mother would take care of me too, so I could feel consideration. My sister's jaundice made her eyes yellow, which acted like a signal, letting my mother know she was sick, and needed attention. I had nothing to signal the need for attention.

My sister cried incessantly for the first five years of her life. Most of the time, I hid in the closet to escape the uproar she made. Later, closets in

Pakistan and Saudi Arabia would become my sanctuaries whenever I needed to hide. My mother later described my unpleasant childhood saying, "I never bathed you, and I cut your hair off so I wouldn't have to comb it."

After I grew older, I surmised she suffered from post-partum depression for the first years of my childhood. I didn't blame her; I blamed my father for allowing his family to treat her with such irreverence.

Around the time my sister turned four, she became my shadow, following me everywhere I went, doing everything I did. My mother sent my sister to a *baba*, or holy man, who supposedly "shredded the jaundice" from her body with his holy broom. Maya and I would run to him every day at 4:00 P.M. Maya truly believed it worked! She survived her jaundice and bad liver problems, but in her eyes remained a tinge of yellow.

By the time I was eight I had no choice but to play the role of part-time mother to my sister; my mother walking around reveling in her self-pity, inconsolable about her inability to conceive a male heir. Her in-laws made it known that the behavior of her womb was unacceptable. They were irate about how she dared conceive two girls!

Throughout that time, my father rarely spent an quality time with my mother, because of his work in

Saudi Arabia. When he returned, his siblings took up most of his time; conversing how he was going to use his pay to help them. Oh, how I wished I was a boy. Maybe then my mother would have awakened from her conscious coma. I know then she would have given me twice the amount of attention she gave my sister. It was from my family I quickly realized the injustices of being a girl in Pakistan.

My father gave me a lot of attention when he came home from Saudi Arabia. Of course I welcomed it, seeing as how I had been insignificant in the house up until that time.

When I reached adulthood, everyone told me how beautiful I was. I had a slim face with eyes that looked like half-moons, full lips, and thick, curly black hair like my mother, with flawless olive skin. As a child, however, I was told I looked like an elephant, because I was larger than all the other girls. I was not sure how I had become so big, but I was sure all my family members thought it was the worst thing in the world for a girl to be so sizable.

I was ridiculed day and night by my family, and those around me. My sanctuary, the closet, was wet with tears of shame and embarrassment whenever I was insulted. My sister would join me in my reclusion, telling me how beautiful I was, which left me sobbing, rather than in hysterics. After she quelled my troubled mind, I found the strength to get out of my sanctuary, and the courage to return to the hazing.

About halfway through my ninth year, my father became very interested in me, showing lots of attention when he came home from Saudi Arabia. Suddenly, I felt accepted and loved. He was a man of Allah, a hard worker, and the sole breadwinner in our house. His special attention was just what I needed to recover my self-esteem.

My father started treating me like a princess during the daytime, and at night, he would tell my mom he was going to sleep on the floor with me. He told my mom, and she agreed. She agreed! I agreed. I was so ecstatic my father wanted to spend time with me. After Maya became well, and my mother's attention was diverted from yearning for a son, I became Maya's savior.

Maya became increasingly obsessed with me, wanting everything my father bought me. She even started talking, walking, and dressing like me. I didn't mind: she was my little gift. The self-confidence my sister gave me would be short-lived, as my mom would rescind her compliments, telling us how "ugly and elephantine" we were, and how hard it would be for her to find husbands for girls so unattractive.

According to western standards, I was not fat, but I was big for my age. At only nine, I weighed 120 pounds, and stood five-feet-five-inches tall. The other Pakistani girls looked like twigs in comparison to me. At age ten, my aunt told me my big hips made me look like I had "birthed ten children already." Through it all, my sister assured me I was beautiful.

My father also complimented me when he came home, watching me throughout the day as if I were a prized thoroughbred. At night, he'd tell me how pretty I was while hugging and kissing me goodnight. Right about then, I started to watch television and saw people, couples who had romantic feelings towards one another, kissing the same way that man kissed me at night. "This is how everyone shows their love to each other," I thought. Back then, I didn't think twice of the kisses, although my lips would swell up and hurt in the morning. I never understood why he needed to put his tongue in my mouth.

Chapter 3
Truly The Home Of Allah

After ten years of going back and forth for work, my father finally grew tired of not having his family around. I suspected his sudden interest in bringing us to Mecca had more to do with his plans for having me around. In all his years he never before offered my mother the opportunity to live in the homeland of Allah.

By 1993, my father decided we were moving to Mecca. He told us he could make more money there by starting his own restaurant selling Indian and Pakistani food, rather than working for others. My mother packed what little we owned, and waited for my father to return with plane tickets. It would be the first time we traveled on a plane.

At age ten, the plane ride from Karachi to Saudi Arabia became the highlight of my life. My grandmother made me a jar of pickled mangoes that opened in our hand luggage and stained most of my clothes. Now, every time I smell pickled mangoes, I remember the intense excitement I felt being on a plane, flying off to somewhere I had never been before. I needed the change of scenery.

My mother and Maya sat across from us, while my father and I sat next to each other on the plane. I had the window seat. I remember holding his hand tight as we lifted off. I was scared, but with my father beside me I felt safe. When the plane landed, the first thing I noticed was the tropical atmosphere, and abundance of plants in comparison to Karachi. Outside the airport, I immediately inhaled the fresh Saudi Arabian air, smiling with Maya as she did the same. In Karachi I had to cover my nose to block the pungent smell of diesel fuel and polluted air.

In Pakistan, we had one streetlight per avenue located at the corner of each block. The big bulb on the pole was just enough for a street guard to see who was going in and out of each neighborhood. The privilege of having street lights and a street guard was exclusive to people in the rich communities. In my neighborhood, and in other slums around town, lights usually hung by the wires down so low they almost touched the streets. This was when they weren't being ripped off, shot, or stoned by thugs and petty thieves who didn't want to see the light.

In Saudi Arabia, there were four to five streetlights per block, and every light had twenty-seven bulbs; I know, because I counted every single bulb from the airport to our new home in Mecca. Soft, yellow lights, shaped like indoor chandeliers, lit up the entire city at night. The street lights were so bright that nighttime became day in Mecca. When my father's uncle came to Mecca from his shanty town in the interior regions of Pakistan, he begged my father to stop the car at each pole, where he bowed in reverence, repeating the words, "Allah-u-Akbar", meaning "Allah is great". Like me, he truly believed Mecca was the home of Allah.

On the dividers of the highways stood miles of flower beds and plants, which were constantly nourished by trucks that watered them religiously.

When we entered the street of the middle-class neighborhood to be our new home, I couldn't help but thank Allah for the bountifulness he was about to provide us. In the back of my mind were vivid memories of visitors to our home back in Pakistan, remarking how small it was.

Every townhouse on that street was at least four to five times bigger than our previous home. I looked across at my father in the air-conditioned car, and couldn't help but hug him when he pointed out the large, four-bedroom, white house that was the size of a mansion.

"This is your new home," he exclaimed while he threw up his hand in the air.

I had to think we had done something really good for Allah to be taken away from the "chicken coop" in Pakistan to this big, wonderful palace.

After we walked through the huge, geometrically shaped, wooden doors, I was awestruck at the ornately furnished, meticulously planned-out house. The kitchen alone was the size of two floors of our house back in Pakistan. At the end of the front hallway was the elaborate living room, with lavish furniture. My parents didn't have a bedroom, they had a wing. There was a second bedroom, which my sister would use sparingly; but just the fact we had more than one room for each of us blew my mind. At the end of the hallway, opposite Maya's room sat mine. We even had an extra guest bedroom.

Across from my bedroom stood a half-bathroom, which only I used to take showers. The other bathrooms were located across from Maya's bedroom and in my parents' room. The kitchen was well equipped, stocked with utensils, dishes, and pots and pans filling up the drawers and cabinets.

My father stood in the entrance to the hallway, smiling in silent acknowledgment of his achievements while I ran from room to room examining each one in awe.

We were all beaming with delight. I must have thanked Allah at least a hundred times that day. My mother went on her knees praising him in the middle of the living room, saying, "Shukur Allah, Shukur Allah, you have rescued me! Masha Allah; I have prayed for this day for so long."

The house was cold from the air conditioner we carelessly and flagrantly turned up to combat the scorching 120-degree temperature outside. When we left the confines of our cooled cocoon during the daytime we felt as if we were about to spontaneously combust at any given moment from the heat. We were accustomed to the heat, because of the similar conditions in Pakistan, but we chose to spare ourselves from the sometimes unbearable temperature, and would only go out in the evening hours, after dark. We adjusted to the change in schedule quickly, and did all our daily activities during the cooler nighttime hours.

My favorite part of the house was the kitchen, which was filled with food I had only dreamt about back in Pakistan. For the next year of my life, I woke up everyday to a full fridge, giving thanks to Allah day and night. It was in that same kitchen where my father began the base for accumulating all his wealth and success by wining and dining the Saudis, and members from the Muttahida Qaumi Movement (MQM), the political party my father worked for.

My father mixed each of the endless spices hailing from India and Bangladesh into the Pakistani/Indian fusion dishes he cooked feverishly around the clock to entertain. He was a magician in the kitchen, and he knew the key to a man's heart was his stomach. He created huge pots of food, loading them into his Toyota Cressida to take to his Saudi friends, and other influential business associates in Saudi society.

I assumed the reason my father did these favors was to gain protection and respect from various authorities. I knew this to be true one Sunday morning at the market. My mother stopped to look at the goods at a vendor's stand. After she asked why the price was so high, the vendor grabbed the item from her and threw it back into his stall saying, "You don't know how to speak English or Arabic, but want to live here, and buy here? Go home and buy there," he scoffed, turning away in disgust.

This made my father furious, and using a piece of wood the size of a cricket bat, he pummeled the vendor into submission. When the police came, the vendor explained what had transpired, blaming my father for the brutality inflicted upon him. When my father started speaking Arabic to the police, telling his side of the story, the police quickly took the vendor into custody, brought him to the police station, and threw him into a cell. At my father's request, the only way he could be released was to apologize for insulting my mother. The man quickly begged to do so, after which the cops freed him.

My father was an organizer for the Muttahida Qaumi Movement, which was the third largest political party in Pakistan at the time. The MQM was against the ruling Pakistan People's Party in Karachi, and had made that known by killing several of its most prominent members. My father organized meetings of the MQM leaders, and followers. These followers were the ones who did the dirty work, including assassins, money laundering, and operating as ministers of propaganda. Saudi Arabia was the safest and most practical place to hide the MQM personnel coming out of Pakistan.

Also, while in Mecca, they could conveniently rid and remove themselves from the sins they committed back home in Pakistan, sometimes hours before they arrived in Mecca. These MQM assassins killed innocent bystanders in the wake of their extermination of members of the opposing Peoples Party, but had no worries: they would be cleansed of their wrongdoings once they performed the pilgrimage to Mecca. My father celebrated in the fact that he was in association with such important and dangerous company.

It was when MQM leaders took asylum in London, however, my father realized the dangers of being a part of this political party. After MQM was associated with terrorist activities, the Pakistani government led a full onslaught against its members. My father quickly burned all the pictures, evidence, and memorabilia from his days when he worshipped the MQM.

Everything we did to glorify the MQM party ended abruptly, becoming a threat to our very survival. We adjusted, forced to adapt once my father told us the leaders of MQM, whose pictures were scattered across our living room walls, were now fugitives in their own country, and political exiles in Saudi Arabia. We took the pictures down, burning them so the wrong person wouldn't see. One of the leaders came to live at our house for a while. Ali was a very religious and somber man. I later found out from him that his son was brutally killed at the hands of the Pakistan Peoples Party's henchmen.

Ali stayed at our home for weeks. He shared with me stories about the death of his son in a poignant voice while looking at the ground saying, "When I found my son, he had bullet holes in his back. They did not have the decency to look him in the face when they snatched his life away. They told him to run, and then they murdered him." I often saw Ali walking around our house with his hand up, as if he were resting it on someone's shoulder, talking as if his son was standing in front of him.

My father was not a part of MQM because he wanted to fight for equal rights and justice in Pakistan; he was a member, because it made him feel he had power, and the respect from those around him to get things done. And, of course, he liked the money the MQM Party provided him.

The Pakistani, Indian, and Bangladesh immigrants around him in Saudi Arabia were only there to stroke his ego. They benefited from all the money he forked over to them for everything from washing his car to working in his restaurant. They surrounded him because he had money; otherwise, he had nothing else to offer. They swallowed their pride when my father threatened them with calling the authorities to report they were working in Saudi Arabia illegally. They were all afraid of him, and he used that fear to do whatever he wanted to make himself look prominent to the Saudis.

Chapter 4
The Awakening

After eleven years of praying in Pakistan, my mother still did not have a son, or the respect of her husband and his family. After three months in Mecca attending Khaana-e-Kaaba, a ritualized prayer every Friday asking for a son, her prayers finally came true.

"Ten years of praying, and I never had a son, and three months after arriving in Mecca I'm pregnant with a boy! This is truly Allah's homeland," she exclaimed after coming from the clinic where she learned the gender of her unborn child.

After Saif was born, mother woke from her conscious coma, completely recovering, and awakening a different person. A year and half later, my youngest brother, Jawad, was also born in Saudi Arabia. She finally had sons.

My mother was now jovial, and ready to take motherhood head-on. Maya and I got whatever leftover attention she could muster after spending countless hours tending to my newborn brothers, spit-shining them like they were a new pair of shoes.

Seemingly as consolation, my brothers didn't get the attention I did from my father, though my mother treated them like they were the president of Pakistan, cooking sumptuous meals for them, toiling away at a frenzied pace breaking almonds and other nutritious foods she claimed gave them "good brains." By then, my sister was the one left out, as my mom now had her sons, and my father gave me all his attention.

It took about a year after my father's restaurant business flourished for us to become noticeably wealthy. With this newfound wealth, my mother decided it was important for us girls to be educated. Since we could afford to get the best, she begged my father to send us to an English-speaking school. Only the man of the house could make such a significant decision in my culture.

We settled for in-house tutoring after my father claimed there were no English or Urdu speaking schools in Mecca. I thanked Allah we were not still in Pakistan. My father's family would never allow us to be educated. Before we left Pakistan, his family asked if my mother was teaching my sister and I, corrupting our minds. They'd sneak up to the third floor to spy, and make certain she wasn't. When my father agreed to allow tutors to come and teach us in our home, she decided it would be English tutors. English was more universal, and she had no plans for us to return to Pakistan, or be confined by Muslim oppression. By the time the first tutor arrived, I had started growing breasts. I covered them with layers of blouses under my burqa so they could not be detected.

It was three days after my tenth birthday that my father told my mother after supper that he was going to sleep in my room. As usual, my mother agreed. I started to feel uncomfortable about my father kissing me the same type of kiss shared between lovers in the movies we watched on Friday nights. The way he kissed me was inappropriate and wrong for a father and daughter. It is only done between people in love, and not the way you love your family: the way you love your wife or husband.

That night changed my life permanently. After everyone fell asleep, my father covered up under the sheets beside me and started kissing me, as usual. About twenty seconds after he started, I felt his hand on my thighs, and seconds later, I felt something hurt very badly in my vaginal area, like a stabbing. I pushed him away with such force that he fell off the bed.

How could this happen in Mecca, the home of Allah? Isn't he supposed to protect me from pain like this? Allah will surely smite this man, striking him down like the animal he is, slaughter him.

Allah must have been sleeping, because no punishment befell my father. Instead, he went right back to it, fondling me. Whatever he did, it hurt like hell. I jumped up to run, to retreat to my sanctuary, and start praying to Allah not to let this man come near me again. It was then he came up to the closet door, and started to whisper.

"My daughter, you should not be scared. Fathers and daughters do this all the time. This is normal."

I didn't believe him. This didn't feel normal, and I refused to come out. Two minutes later, he finally forced the door open.

"I won't do it again, but don't tell anyone. This is our secret. If you tell anyone it will destroy our family will, and we will end up like Aunty Seema's family." Her daughter, Abeera, had merely hinted that her father had tried to touch her inappropriately, and that accusation was enough to have her father extracted from the household. Exiled to Bahrain, he wasn't seen for many years.

After that insinuation, my male cousins relentlessly beat their sister, charging her with lying about their father, their role model. Only twelve, she, the accuser, went insane, secluding herself, and talking as if possessed by evil spirits. She lost her mind, unable accept what a father had done to his own daughter.

Not long after, Abeera became obsessed with a married man three times her age. She claimed to be mesmerized by him, and could not live without him. Aunty Seema had to commit her to a psychiatric institution in Islamabad to prevent her from seeing him. My aunt stood strong, trying to keep her family together, but this was a man's world, and when her sons were grown they overpowered her, bringing their father back into the home.

Everything seemed fine after he came back, but I felt sorry for my little cousin, as she never recovered from the trauma she endured. Now twenty-three, she lives her life in purgatory. She will never marry, or have a normal life, and even worse: she has to look at her molester's face every day. I only hear stories about her from my mother telling me how she tries to free herself by suicide.

My father's entry into my bedroom that fateful night was the beginning of the end of my happy life. That man would take every ounce of the pride I somehow managed to gain, despite my family's constant scrutiny of my weight. The ironic thing is some of that confidence emanated from listening to him, and my sister, talk about my good looks. After that night, I lived among the *badroohs*, or evil spirits, and during the day, I walked lifelessly, not being able to be myself, detached from the world, in denial about what was happening to me.

Night after night at the dinner table, surrounded by his family, that man would tell his wife, in front of his children, he would be spending the night in my room, leaving me nauseated, scared, and trembling from the time of the announcement to the time we were finished cleaning up after supper, and ready to go to bed. I counted every second on the clock, tucked under my covers, watching the light under the door, waiting for the shadows; until he showed up. I knew he was coming to take another piece of my soul, but I couldn't bring myself to cry out. Who could I cry out to? Who would hear me? He told my mother bluntly, and she refused to listen.

I guessed she was under the same evil spell the warlock had placed upon me. Like myself, she was not able to blame him. He swore he was a disciple of Islam, and a good Muslim who would never do anything to hurt his family, or harm us in any way. Make no mistake: I was afraid of my family ending up like Aunty Seema's.

Night after night he would go a little further with his twisted experiment, which he justified by calling it "showing me love." Every time I thought about telling my mother, I remembered his warning about Aunty Seema's family: "Don't let that happen to our family." My mom was finally recovering from depression with the birth of my two brothers-I couldn't let her know what was happening. It would have certainly sent her over the edge to the madhouse. At the time, I thought her mental state was so fragile I would have to silently take the abuse, waiting until she was stronger to tell her about the transgressions of her husband.

One night, he put his wretched finger inside me, with a warning not to tell anyone. He told me to relax: he was going to make me "feel good." While I lay there motionless, I transported into some sort of trance, removing myself, out of my own body as he took off my underwear, and started kissing my navel. Down he went, licking me with his tongue along the way. I squirmed involuntarily, my body reacting to the sensation. He started licking me as if he were a camel drinking water from an oasis.

I was in shock this time around, because what he did wasn't painful. It felt tingly, as when he used to tickle me until I couldn't take anymore, and the euphoria of laughing too much took over my entire being. That night was more confusing, and concerning. How could I feel good about something I knew was so wrong? How could I have felt that way? What did that say about me? What did that man do to me?

How could I betray my mother by feeling pleasure from such terrible acts? I would have to tell her! I would have to let her know about the evil spell that had been cast upon us. *He will leave for the restaurant in the morning*, I told myself, and I would pray Allah allow a truck to hit him on the way home so I would never have to feel this way again.

When daylight came, I would look into my mother's eyes to see if she saw the shame on my face. I was sure the tutors and everyone around me saw it. I spent the entire next day in the house, unable to pay attention to anything. I could not understand what had happened to me. It was disastrous! I started to look down and away from people. I know Maya suspected something because she kept asking me what was wrong. She toiled all day, asking me, "*Baji*, what's happened to you?" I did not notice it, but Maya saw my lips were swollen from how hard he kissed me.

Maya could see it, how could my own mother not know? Knowing how my sister loved to gossip with our cousins, I didn't dare trust her with the truth at that time. How could I tell her the man she looked up to was a warlock who used his sorcery on me at night, forcing his will upon me? I had no choice! I kept it inside, hidden from my entire family.

Two days passed without that monster visiting my room, but on the third night, during dessert, he was going to watch the film *Ghost* in my room with me. My sister immediately announced she wanted to watch also, but he quickly refused, shooting down her self-imposed invitation. He told my mother that the younger children were to go to bed at their regular time; he was staying up with me because I was the oldest. Again, the trance came over me like the darkness of night over the caves that filled the mountains behind our house.

Chapter 5
Night Class

Not long after my mother and siblings went to bed, the sorcerer came into my room, holding a plastic bag of videocassettes, with a crazed look in his eyes. He pressed play, then sat on the bed beside me without saying a word. The movie was poor quality, but I could see everything. An old Indian man and a girl talked to each other in what appeared to be a spa. Then they started kissing. The actor started to do everything to the girl that my father had done to me the nights before.

While the movie played, my father continuously said, "This man in the movie is the girl's father. Look, *mera bacha:* look how much she loves her father. *Mera bacha mujhe bhi ese hi pyaar kare ga na.* Why can't my child love me like that too?"

I did not believe the sorcerer, because if this behavior were normal, aunty Seema would not have banished her husband from their house. I remember a time she loved him too much. It killed her to see him leave-but he had to go. I was so ashamed. I felt like walking down into the kitchen, and plunging one of my mother's butcher knives into my chest. I turned away in disgust after seeing the images on the screen. My father suddenly grabbed me by my hair and said, in a stern voice, "You'd better watch so you can learn."

When I looked at the television again, the girl had placed the man's penis in her mouth and proceeded to suck as if she were getting sweet mango juice from it. The tape went on for about ten minutes more. I remember thinking, *"why would I need to learn this?"* I barely finished that thought when my father started something new on me. He kissed my breasts while holding my hands at my side. I tried to move away, but to no avail. He was too overpowering that night.

He kissed and licked my breasts until I once again became euphoric, as I had been the night before.

Throwing me down, he climbed on top of my chest, unzipped his pants, pulling out his penis, and grabbing my mouth. I tried so hard to keep my mouth shut, but I was weakened by too many nights of assaults, and whatever other sorcery he had done to my body. After a couple of minutes, he climbed off me, and started masturbating. When he was done he turned away, and faced the window of my room, looking out into the starry distance. Grabbing my blouse I made a dash to the door, then raced to my mother's room, thinking he would not be able to do those despicable acts to me in front of her. He never followed me into that room.

After realizing the warlock was not in pursuit, I went to the bathroom to wash my face, and rinse my mouth with soap. After I finished washing, I returned to my mother's side, searching for refuge. My youngest brother was already residing in that spot, so I moved him to create space. This activity woke my mother from her sleep, and she turned to look at me as if I were crazy. I lay behind her, hugging her tightly, hoping that somehow she would feel my fear, and ask me what was wrong. I shook her when I realized she was falling back asleep, but she looked at me, irritated, and went back to her slumber.

I felt dirty, used, and out of control. I was scared, disgusted, and couldn't stop myself from recalling the euphoric feeling I felt. The next day, I walked around the house feeling I betrayed my mother, just as my father had done.

I also remember feeling a mixture of jealousy and anger towards my mother when I heard them having sex at night. The next morning, I asked her what she had done the night before.

"For years I had to listen to your father's family asking me about my private doings," she said in anger, "and now you? Get away from me."

I could not tell her what transpired between her husband and me, because she would surely think I was to blame. The next day, my little sister tirelessly asked me to play with her dolls. I smacked them away from her, growling like a rabid dog. I begged her to leave me alone, but she would not, and when she asked me what was wrong, I started crying uncontrollably, and ran to my sanctuary. It was lunchtime, around 3:00 P.M., when my mother came knocking at the closet door, inquiring what happened to me. I could not answer, and kept bawling uncontrollably. She finally left me alone after few minutes, putting no extra effort into finding out what was bothering her eldest child.

When the tutor arrived at our home, my mother sent him away, saying I was not feeling well. I missed lunch and dinner that day because I refused to leave the closet. At night, I went to bed and slept all night, but when morning came, I couldn't get out of bed. The next night, after my family retired to bed after supper, I became crammed with anxiety. The nauseous feelings in my stomach continued to plague me.

I waited for him to come through the door, which I barricaded with the dresser-but he didn't show up that night. The next morning, while my mother prepared breakfast I removed the dresser, and lay back in bed while my mother begged for my help cooking. I must have fallen back asleep to escape the reality I stayed up al night facing. Suddenly, I was awakened by something brushing against my cheek. We had centipedes roaming around the house, and though I had never seen one crawling around in my bedroom, I assumed that is what the contact was with. I swiped at my face feverishly, but it was not a centipede.

It was a man rubbing his penis against my face and lips! I jumped up so hard my head flew back, crashing into the wooden headboard of my bed. He put his finger by his lips, signaling me to keep quiet, then motioned to the kitchen where my mother was cooking breakfast. He climbed up in the bed, sticking his filthy penis in my mouth. I remember as if it were yesterday. It was a Friday, the day we usually dressed up and went to the mosque. Men dressed in their best shalwar and qameez(pants and shirt), and women went in their finest burqas, only showing their eyes to the rest of the world. I would tell my mother I didn't want to go to the mosque, but my father forced me out of the house, slapped me on my face, and yelled, "Go pray to Allah."

I remember praying, "Allah, I pray to you take this man out of my life, or take my life. Where are you, Allah? Where is Prophet Muhammad? Someone, hear my cry!"

I prayed that evening for hours-the same words over and over. I looked at my father while he prayed beside me outside the mosque to see if he had an ounce of remorse in his bones for what he had done to me and his family. I saw nothing in his expression but pride and wickedness. The more I prayed and asked Allah to show me a way out, the more empty and lost I felt. There was no answer. I thought right then and there my father would burst into a ball of fire for praying to Allah in a mosque after what deeds he had committed.

I also remember thinking to myself, maybe Allah is on vacation on one of those pretty islands-but when Allah finally gets back, and his angel tells him about these insidious, incestuous acts, he will light my father aflame right before my very eyes. Would

Allah do the same to me? After all: I had committed a sin too!

When my father did those things to my body, I felt tingly, and sometimes good. I hated myself even more that day in the mosque. I was just like the infidel! I was just like that warlock! I did not want to roam this earth any longer!

After about three weeks of begging for Allah to do something, nothing continued to happen. I surmised Allah must never have returned from vacation. However, this was Mecca, the homeland of Allah, and he *had* to return and see what was happening to me! He never answered my prayers.

Two weeks after forcing me to watch porn and perform oral sex on him, my father came into my bedroom once again. He sat on my bed with one leg on the bed, and the other on the ground. Then, he began to talk.

"I love your mother, and I love you. Right now you may not like this, but you will see it is for your own good. When you get married, you will really know how to please your husband, but never tell him how you learned," he said, putting his hands on my head, pushing me down. He began to tell me in detail how he masturbated for two years watching his younger sister in the shower. He told me how he planned it for months, then one day cunningly waited to "make love" to her in the shower when his mother and father took their brothers to the market.

"She loved it," he said, smiling, "She was different after that. She was so pretty and cute. She often snuck into my bedroom to make love to me after that day..."

I knew he was lying when he said she loved it. My aunt, his sister he raped, was the only one of his eight siblings who never came to our house. On special occasions, like marriages, she would show up, but she avoided him as though he were an infectious disease.

After telling me the story about him and his sister, my father left the room. I was so relieved. The apprehension in my stomach subsided after he left. I went to the kitchen to get something to eat. As soon as I returned to my room I dropped my plate of food at the sight of him in my bed in his underwear.

"Allah, please stop this evil," I yelled. "Get out!"

This is the first time I resisted, and voiced any opposition. Something must have come over me that night. He jumped from my bed, and slapped me so hard I was sure my mother, who should have heard the uproar, would head to my room at any moment. The only new addition to the room were the tears rolling down my face.

"You want to cry? I'll give you a reason to cry!"

He took off his shoe and started pounding the top of my head with it. He snarled, his teeth protruding from his mouth, biting his lower lip, his eyes glaring, nostrils flaring like those of a raging bull. He continued beating me with his shoe until his arm became fatigued. My mother never came to my rescue, and there I was—left unprotected at the hands of the beast, unable to flee!

He stopped hitting me, and yelled for me to be quiet. Without hesitation, he took my clothes off, and started kissing me everywhere. The tears kept streaming down except, unlike before, I could not feel a thing. He had never hit me before, except one time when I was young, and beat up my little brother.

The pain I felt that night was immense. He stopped kissing me, stood up, and motioned at me to suck his penis. Reluctantly, I did. Unlike the other nights, he masturbated while I did it, ejecting what looked like yogurt all over the side of my bed. I was shocked and mortified! For months, I could not eat anything remotely resembling yogurt, and twice I threw up when I saw my sister eating it. When he was finished, he fell on the bed as though he had suffered a heart attack, saying, "I love you, *Baji*." He took a towel, and cleaned off my bed, telling me, "This is how you should make a man feel, *Baji*!" He stared at me for a minute then left as swiftly as he had entered.

The next morning I woke feeling numb, brain-dead, and unable to rise out of bed. My mother came to my room, asking if I was sick again. I told her "yes", as usual. She came to my room several mornings after that, inquiring why I consistently could not get out of bed. She rubbed my head, running her fingers through my hair, then brought me breakfast. Afterwards, she returned to her room to pray. Later, my sister entered the room, asking if I was okay.

"*Baji*, are you sick again?" she asked softly.

Looking at her I sprang up out of bed, grabbed her by the hair, and began drubbing her face the way my mother used to beat meat when making kabobs. What instigated the onslaught Maya calling me "*Baji*" as my father had the night before. I did not stop beating her until my mother dragged me off her.

What have I done? I was overcome with guilt once I became aware of my behavior. I looked at my sister's face, which was swollen from the pounding my fists had given it, but Maya didn't cry. My mother yelled at me, but I was so astonished by my actions I could not hear what she was saying. I was not myself-I was possessed. That man had turned me into a wild animal capable of beast-like behavior.

I loved my sister, but she had chosen the wrong word to use that morning. She followed me around all day, showing me even more love than she usually did. I figured she thought I didn't love her anymore, so I did what she loved best, and all day we played with the Barbie and Ken dolls given to us by my mother's sister who lived in the United States. While playing in her bedroom, I told her I was sorry for what I did.

"What is happening to you, Laila?" she asked.

I started crying, and told her I was losing my mind. I also repeated several times that I loved her and was very, very sorry for what I had done. Maya was very smart, and I remember thinking she must know something is askew. She must have seen the disgrace on my face.

While Maya asked question after question, I wondered why she was so persistent. Was it because it had happened to her? No, I decided. I had to believe that. Maya never left my mom's side at night. I guessed my father to big a coward to do anything with my sister in the same bed as her. Perhaps she had been awakened by the ruckus. Did she see how humiliated I felt? Why did my mom not feel the same? Why didn't Allah show her what was happening to me?

She walked around the house every day, cooking and cleaning, and when the Bengali maid came to clean and wash our clothes, she sat and talked with the maid's daughter. Why she did not sit and talk to me? I remember thinking my father had done something to make her not able to notice or discern what was happening to me.

I started to believe my father had powers given to him by the evil spirits he worshipped. He prayed to Allah and was a devoted Muslim, so I wondered who was giving him this power to do those unspeakable acts to his own daughter. I swore it could not be Allah.

My love for my mother lessened every day thereafter. After more than a year of those nightly visits, I became more and more comfortable with what was happening to me. I became a disgusting animal that sometimes enjoyed the way my father touched me. I hated myself so badly that sometimes I randomly banged my head against the nearest wall- and some of the time I lay there numb, counting the number of rotations the ceiling fan made.

Chapter 6
The Hajj Pilgrims

By age thirteen, I became a half-dead, a lost soul without one, who wanted to check out completely from this world. I stumbled out of bed every afternoon around 1:00 P.M., to feed myself, and pretend to want to live among others. The nights brought video cassettes of Indian girls having sex with men who looked three times their age — and my father performing oral sex on me.

Every night, he left the tapes playing, my mind broken, warning me not to speak a word. Around 2:00 P.M. the next day, the new tutor came over to teach us English. My mom had fired the first one, a younger tutor, who taught English and math, after I complained he was insolent and perverted. One day, adjusting my *dupatta*, or scarf, it fell off my shoulders. "Don't worry: I have seen what you are hiding," he said, holding my wrist in his hands, and pulling me closer to him. I stood my ground that day, yelling out my mother's name.

I started to believe every man in the world was like my father, and what he did was nothing different from what any man would do, given the opportunity. All I did that year was watch pornography. I was not afraid of the tutors-they could not harm me during the daytime while mother did her chores, buzzing around us like a bee to a flower. After that incident, she only hired tutors who were old men over sixty years old.

Nights after the indecent tutor was fired my father came into my room for his nightly sessions. I asked if every man was the way he was.

"Why do you ask this question?" he inquired.

I replied by telling him the details of the tutor's wrongdoings. He immediately walked out of the room, and into the bedroom where my mother and sister slept. He shook my mother awake.

"Why didn't you tell me about dirty the tutor?" he yelled at her. Ammi never answered.

I started to pray to Allah for a solution after my father left. Allah must have heard my cry, because the next day my mother rushed out of the house, asking me to take care of my siblings while she was gone. She never told me where she was going, but I later found out she had been summoned to the local police station by the Bengali cook who worked at my father's restaurant.

I loved my father unconditionally throughout my childhood. When my mother's family described him as an uneducated loser I became furious, cursing them. I waited by the door of our house every day at 3:00 P.M. to listening for the sound of his keys jingling to unlock it. I always thought highly of him, even after he raped me. This time around, I was happy he was in trouble, and I thought what he had done was unacceptable.

Apparently, he had done something really bad, because people were coming to our house looking for him the next day. What he did was unconscionable in Mecca. He had stolen from the *Hajj* people. They were Muslims from all over the world who go on pilgrimage to Mecca. They had paid my father in advance to procure food and livestock for them, including two thousand goats for the celebration.

The custom is to kill a goat, sheep, or camel as a sacrifice to Allah on the fifth and last day of *Hajj*, the day following Abraham's trials. One-third of the meat is eaten immediately, the rest donated to the poor. My father had no intention of giving those people their food and livestock. Instead, he hid the money at his friend's house. I wondered how anyone could do that to those *Hajj* pilgrims-and in Mecca of all places. He would have to be the worst kind of person.

When they arrested my father, my mother checked their bank accounts, but saw no significant changes. Later on, however, the friend holding the money told my mother how the police brought my father to his house, shackled like a slave, chains linked around his ankles, wrists, and neck. The friend quickly handed over the money to the police.

Chapter 7
Fugitives in Mecca

My father was sentenced to one year in a Saudi prison. He later told my mother that the guards at the prison gave him a hundred lashes as a part of his punishment. My father's friends were embarrassed by his shameful act, so they never came to our house to help us when we were in need. We were outcasts in the homeland of Allah. We were scared, not knowing if we would be arrested or killed for being his family. We thought those *Hajj* pilgrims were going to come to our house, drag us out, and stone us to death.

We had a small hole in the front of the house where a broken air conditioner used to be. The *Hajj* pilgrims' henchmen tried unsuccessfully to come through the hole several times.

We were prisoners in our own home, and within weeks, we were scrounging for food. We had no choice but to send word back home to Pakistan, begging my mother's brother for money and plane tickets out of Mecca. We were so afraid to leave the house to go to the airport that we made a mad dash from the house to the waiting cab at 3:00 A.M., using the dark of night for concealment to escape out of the city. We made it to the airport, bringing with us a few pieces of clothing, which we carried in small bags, leaving everything else behind.

On the plane ride to Pakistan I swore it was Allah answering my prayers to rid me of the improprieties in my life. I had imagined the day when I would have peace in my heart, never thinking that day would come, but I was wrong.

Reality hit me like a barrel of crude oil. What I had prayed for turned out not to be in the best interest of my family. We had grown accustomed to the good life. We had everything in Mecca. We had Bangladeshi helpers and drivers, had the best materials used to make our clothes, and enjoyed an abundance of delectable food.

All the great foods I ate in Mecca made me plump, but I still looked beautiful, because my face and neck remained slim. All the extra pounds rested on my hips, tummy, and breasts.

On the plane I grew terrified, worrying about my family, and dreading how I would be teased by everyone in Pakistan. What would happen to my brothers, sister, and me? Fearing starvation and poverty, I again turned to Allah: this time for my father's release. The saddest part of all was realizing I missed him.

What kind of crazy person had I become? Why would I have feelings for someone who betrayed the sanctity and trust of a daughter-father relationship? Yet, I still loved him. Those sinful acts would not be easily washed away.

My mother, who sat beside me in the plane, started crying for my father, but I dared not shed a tear. For the entire flight, I thought I should have bitten off his penis when I had the chance. Man of Allah? No way! He was pure evil! I was grateful for one thing: my sister would be safe from him now.

Chapter 8
Hell in Pakistan

Maya said nothing throughout the flight, but began nervously asking questions when the plane landed in Karachi. She was anxious, not knowing our destiny, and recognizing we were in trouble. In the past, several times I shared with her how lucky we were to be living in Saudi Arabia. When she visited Pakistan, she always pleaded with my mother to take her back.

"Are we going to buy a new air conditioner?" she asked softly, forgetting what life was like back here. She was obviously worried about the temperature of our grandmother's house, which was usually as hot as the big pit in the kitchen she used to bake bread in. My father's brother, Zafar, who reluctantly paid for our plane tickets, waited for us outside the airport.

Uncle Zafar deprived my mother a house of her own. My father started building it, but before we left for Mecca, my uncle took it to start his business of his own. He used the profits to buy a house of his own, where he brought us to live. He wanted to give the illusion of a happy, devout Muslim home, but I was not happy. Along with my mother telling me how poorly my father's family had treated her, I also remembered how terribly they treated me as a child. This was not the escape I imagined when I prayed to Allah to solve my problems.

The abuse was endless for the next three weeks, as we became the family's personal slaves: cleaning their house, washing their clothes, cooking their food, and bathing their children. In return for our diligence, we were chastised for using the fan to cool ourselves in 105-degree temperatures, given minimal food, and generally frowned upon. They physically abused us children by wringing our ears whenever they perceived us to be stepping out of line.

My brothers had been spoiled rotten by my mother, and were too young to adjust to the culture shift. About four weeks after we arrived, Uncle Zafar beat my little brother's so hard he started to bleed. I unleashed the anger I felt toward my father on him, punching, kicking, and screaming before blacking out.

The family believed I was possessed, and that my family would pay the price for my sudden bout of courage. We were going to be homeless. Zafar threw us out of his house, leaving us no choice but to live in my grandmother's, squeezing into her two-bedroom house in the Buffer Zone of Karachi.

My mother was severely depressed by the time we arrived at my grandmother's house, spending most of her days lying lifeless on the couch in the living room staring at the television screen, and once again: I became the mother to my siblings. I cooked what little food we had during the day, and at night, I bathed them, and brushed their hair and teeth. My sister needed special attention to help cope with her advancing depression. Maya was not used to sleeping on the ground, or not eating for days at a time, both of which she could've dealt with if only she'd been given access to an air conditioner. The suffocating atmosphere at night of being packed like sardines into a tiny tin of a room in over one hundred-degree temperature was unbearable for all of us, but Maya took it the hardest. One night she woke up screaming. She disappeared from the house for hours at a time, often to be found sitting on the roof, staring at the sky, or watching the neighborhood children play cricket on the streets below. Her skin became dark like the Bengalis who washed cars in the sun all day back in Saudi Arabia.

I started talking to Maya more and more, using my family as my relief. After her mood changed for the better, we started keeping each other in check, making sure we didn't lose our minds.

No one came to visit us, no one came to help us. My mother had twelve gold bangles she received in Saudi Arabia as gifts. Never wearing them in public, we hardly saw them, but we knew she had them hidden safely. In Saudi Arabia she would clean them, telling us, "They're yours when you get married." They must have been worth a lot, because they were enough to buy us food for the next few months. My grandmother, Nani, who was my mother's mother, also helped us. She was also a big believer in education. She loved teaching so much she rose to the ranks of headmistress at the high school in near her home.

Each day when school ended I hurried home to prepare dinner. The new school was not a good fit for me. I grew to detest the sight of the school's imposing metal gates, which looked like the front of a prison.

The first day I walked into class, everyone stared at me as if I were an alien. I was the tallest, and biggest, girl in school, so I was teased mercilessly on a daily basis. My self-esteem was lower than the dirt I dragged my feet across. I looked at myself as fat, evil, and not worthy. Maya tried hard to keep me happy, but memories, mixed with reality, were too potent.

Plagued by what happened to me in Mecca, I had nightmares of waking up to my father demanding sex. I thought about what I had seen on the videotapes, and how what I had been forced to watch excited me-and then I became angry that I was excited. What made me hate myself more is the fact I actually missed it. Sometimes I felt my mind would explode from all the confusion. I had a secret I could not tell. I wished there were something I could do to purge my soul. Failing my classes, due to suffering from severe anxiety, every aspect of my life was becoming a nightmare. Furthermore, about six months after school started, my mother announced my father had been released from jail, and was heading to Pakistan.

That night the concoction of emotions overloaded my body and brain until I became physically ill, vomited up my dinner. Despondency overtook my being at the thought of the things he had done, but I became thankful we would not have to live in poverty much longer.

That man is a con artist, and, despite his faults, would find a way to provide for us. He would surely take the house back from uncle Zafar, and make it our home, like the one we had in Mecca, and mother would return to reality, and stop sleeping her life away.

She seemed very happy with the news of my father's return. She cooked and cleaned like never before, and when she was done, I watched her thread all the extra hair that had overtaken her once beautifully manicured face and body like an overgrown rose garden.

My brothers were so happy they could not control themselves. They hugged him for what seemed an hour when he walked in the door. My sister, on the other hand, much like myself, did not seem so excited about his return. He sat at the dinner table where mother and I prepared his favorite foods: *haleem* (beef in oats), *biryani* (chicken and rice), and curried goat meat. He ate as though he had not had food in years.

I sat in the corner of kitchen watching him eat, wondering what his return meant for me, and my future. He looked at me from across the room, then summoned me to come give him a hug. I could not move, my mind blank, my body cold. Next thing I knew, my mom came over, and grabbed my hand to make me give my father a hug. Somehow, I gathered enough strength to make my way to the table.

He grabbed me by my waist, and said, "Did you miss me?" I could not answer. The answer to that question bothered me, and weighed on my mind every day of my life.

Had he known I would miss him? My mother interrupted, startling me by saying, "Your father is talking to you, little girl!"

"Yes," I answered, surprised I actually meant it, and was not just saying it to appease him. When bedtime came we all retired to one crammed, cramped bedroom. *At least nothing will happen tonight*, I thought. Oh, how wrong I was.

After everyone fell asleep, I felt a poke in my side. It was him! He pointed to my mother, who was still sleeping, then whispered to me, "Shh..." The streetlight outside streamed through the window, and lit up the room, allowing me to see everything that transpired.

He proceeded to take my mother's clothes off, waking her fro her once peaceful rest. He kissed her breasts and neck, and kept going, doing the things to her I had seen on the video cassettes he made me watch months before. She laid there motionless while he did what he wanted with her. When he was done, she drew her clothes back on and went back to sleep as quickly as she had been awakened. To this day I don't understand why I watched. I found myself wanting him to do the same things with me. I was a sick, confused girl who was slowly going insane with her perverted thoughts.

It was not long after she had fallen back asleep that he climbed over my two brothers, and lay beside me. He noticed my breasts had grown, and fondled them with glee, saying, "Wow, *Baji*, you're even sexier now!"

When he started kissing my breasts, it invoked feelings I'd never felt before. He climbed on top of me the way he did my mother, and put his finger inside me. When I looked over at my sister's sleeping face, I pushed him as hard as I could to get him off me, only to have him climb back on, unable to take "no" for an answer. This time he kissed me with such strength and passion my lips started to hurt. I sank into a hole in my mind, and blacked out as I lay there helpless.

The next thing I knew his penis was inside me. I lay there lifeless while he humped away with my sister, brothers, and mother sleeping right beside me. After I looked at them, I felt such pity for myself and my family that I wanted was for all of us to be dead.

I will surely kill myself tomorrow, I thought. I will pretend to be sick, not go to school, and cut my throat. I felt a liquid oozing out of me. My father hopped off, went back beside his wife, and fell right asleep. I was fourteen! I was a child!

I ran to the bathroom, crying so much my eyes became stained red, and bloodshot. When I turned the lights on I realized the liquid I felt oozing from my body was blood running down my legs. I felt nauseated, frightened, and almost fainted. I did not know what was happening. I realized the blood could possibly be on the sheets lining the cot I slept on. Running back towards the room my legs felt soaked in blood. When I reached the door of the room my knees buckled, and I collapsed.

What was I going to tell them: my father just raped me, and now I was bleeding to death?

I decided I would go to my grandmother's room. When I entered, she was not asleep, but my presence startled her. "What do you want child?" she asked in a disgusted voice. "Do you know it is 3:30 A.M.?"

As I walked in slowly she leaned over to the lamp on the nightstand beside her bed, and switched it on while fishing for her glasses. Immediately, she saw the tears and anguish on my face. She summoned me to come closer, and looked deep into my eyes, as though they would tell her why I had come to her room. I felt blood trickling from my crotch in little droplets, and looked down to see if it was noticeable.

Her eyes followed mine, and by the time I looked back up, our eyes met.

"Did your mother not tell you about this day?" she asked.

Her question frazzled me. Did my mother know this was happening? Did Nani? What the hell! Was this some big joke on me? Was this to be expected? All these questions ran concurrently through my mind.

Then she spoke in a soft voice, "You are a woman now. This is called menstruation. The blood you see will come every month around the same time. This means you are now able to have children."

Was I going to have a baby with my father? Was this bleeding going to continue until I got pregnant? Did Nani not know what my father was doing? I started to cry again.

She took me in her arms, wiping the blood from my legs with a towel. It was less than I had thought. She reiterated to me this was all part of growing up. She said the blood came naturally. Back then I thought she was as evil as my father, and this was a conspiracy to make me my father's second wife. There he was—pillaging my childhood, and she was telling me this was normal.

I became completely engulfed in the idea that my mother and grandmother knew what was happening, and more importantly, were happy about it. After all, my father told me about the sister he "made love" to, and his family was seemingly fine with that. His elder brother tried to rape my mother, and his family seemed to accept that easily too.

After an hour I stopped crying, prompting Nani to leave me in the bathroom, smiling as she closed the door. "Are you going to be okay, child?"

"Yes," I answered as she shut the door, thinking the devil was going to enter at any minute. I needed to get out of the bathroom to keep everyone from knowing what happened. Somehow, all the self-pity and self-hatred left my body. After washing my face I walked out, and went into the room where everyone slept. I hesitated at the door before pushing it open, and peeking in to make sure no one was awake. Everyone, including my father was still asleep. It made me sick to see him cuddling with my mother, hugging her tightly, as if he loved her.

Traitor! Traitor! You betrayed all of us, and robbed me of my childhood!

Hurrying in, I took my soiled sheets, and brought them to the kitchen door that led out back. I would have to go out in the darkness, and walk about fifty feet to the nearest group of rocks behind my house. I would have to stash them there until the daytime when I could wash them. I was so scared that my body nearly went limp when I opened the door. I sat at the kitchen table forever going over my plan in my mind for anything that might trip it up. I remembered how inquisitive my siblings were, and was petrified one of them might wake up, and see me deliberating in the kitchen, sheets in hand.

Quickly I leapt up, and ran as fast as I could to the rocks. The black scorpions we always saw scampering across the formation just before the sun went down scurried across my mind. *Please, Allah, protect me.* I placed my hand in between the two biggest rocks and jammed the sheets into the crack.

Making a mad dash back to the house I closed the kitchen door behind me, and almost fainted when I turned to see my mother standing there waiting for me. She had woken up to make herself some tea and noticed something was amiss.

"What are you doing child?" she said in a caring, not accusatory voice. "Why are you outside in the middle of the night?"

Lying to her was the easy part. After all, I'd been hiding the truth from her for almost five years.

"I was trying to catch some fireflies," I said in the most innocent-sounding voice I could muster.

"Fireflies?"

"Yes, fireflies."

"Don't go out there at night," she demanded. "There are men who walk through the yard to get to end of the block where the prostitutes live. They will take you away!"

You know and warn me about the men who walk through the yard at night, but you don't know about the man in our home who has robbed me of my childhood! I wanted to tell her she was a poor excuse for a mother, but I said nothing.

I walked away in disgust, and was soon back in the sleeping room. I tried to get close to my sister, as I had no longer had sheets to cover myself with. Once she realized I was behind her, Maya tugged at every inch of the cloth, as if I had come to rob her of her most prized possession. She grabbed and yanked until there was nothing left for me. At least I was thankful it was almost impossible for the sorcerer to do to Maya the things he did to me. She was usually stuck to my mother like the leeches I saw on cows' feet.

My mom re-entered the room and saw I didn't have any sheets. She went into her closet and handed me the new sheets she had received from her sister. They were soft cotton, which felt like heaven compared to the dingy, old, polyester sheets I had just hidden. Wrapping up, and covering myself in the soft fabric I drifted to sleep.

Why did my mom not ask me where my sheets were? What was wrong with that woman? At least my Nani thought I was having my period. What was my mother's excuse? Did she know? That question plagued me until I was twenty-five years old.

Chapter 9
Evil Has No Boundaries

I remember as though it were yesterday when my father came back home from Islamabad, the capital of Pakistan, with that smug look on his face. He had gone there to pick up the visa he applied for two days before at the United States Embassy. I knew for sure he was leaving to go to the U.S., and asked myself why he was so happy to go to a place so evil. I justified it with the fact that any man filled with as much evil as him belonged with the rest of the infidels, and would fit right in.

Hell: he would love it there! It had only been a matter of time before the two nefarious entities came together.

"How far is it?" I asked my grandmother. She told me he would probably need not only one, but two jumbo jets to get there.

"One from here to Europe, then one from Europe to America," she said.

"Far enough for me to be free from this infidel!" I yelled, running to the backyard in jubilation. A sudden peace reigned over my body like cool air on a steamy Pakistani day. "Allah has rescued me once again." The only other time I felt like that was the day my father was imprisoned. I only hoped this joy would not turn bittersweet like last time.

I felt melancholy for my mother and brothers, because of how much they loved him, and how much I loved them. I knew in my heart I would miss that man too, even after everything he had done, yet I wanted Allah to have a Karachi cab driver strike him down in the street like a dog. There was something psychotic going on inside my head that I would have to recover from somehow.

Around dinnertime, I slipped away to the bathroom to pray to Allah about the new events that would bring change, and hopefully peace, to my family. I immediately knelt down in front of the shower and started to pray:

"Allah, you know my heart. You know my fears and my strengths, what I have done, and what has been done to me — if there is anything sinful in my heart or mind, I want you to cut it out, and erase it. I won't make it if these feelings continue plaguing me. I will take my life, Allah. I am supposed to hate sin: how could I miss the man who has committed the most sinful acts towards me? I am just as sinful, Allah? If I am, cut me down where I stand."

I waited in the bathroom for a bolt of lightning to strike me, or the bus that ran on my street to come tearing through the walls and smite me right there in the bathroom-but nothing happened. I waited about ten minutes until I heard my mother beckoning me to help her cook dinner. Tears covered my face, so I washed them away, and put my shoes back on. Opening the bathroom door I felt empty and hollow. I knew then that Allah was not listening to me. I walked slowly to the kitchen, and went to the counter where I started making dough for *nan* beside my mother, already cutting up onions to caramelize.

I felt my mother staring at me from the side, so I quickly turned away from her, and looked in the direction of the *tandoor* hole in the ground. I had not looked my mother in the face since the first time my father put his hands on me. I felt I had betrayed her in so many ways that I could not. I must have been in a daze while she called my name, because it took a sharp slap on the back to knock me out of it.

"Why are you not answering me? Do you think I don't deserve an answer?"

For the first time in months I turned, and looked at her. I needed to look into her eyes to see if she had seen my degradation-or if somehow she knew what transpired only inches away from her. I stared at her huge, dark brown eyes forever until she slapped me upside the head.

"Answer me!" she demanded.

I felt both love and hate looking into her eyes-so wide open, yet still so blind. The only thing she saw were the needs of the boys in my family. "Yes," I answered, "I'm sorry for daydreaming."

My mother looked at me for an eternity, trying to see through me, before turning away, and continuing to prepare the food.

Allah, I am going to explode with this guilt! "Ammi!" I cried out.

She turned, shocked at the tone of my voice, my lips moving, but no sounds or words came out. *He's done terrible things...don't miss him when he is gone...*Those words were being produced by my brain, but not my mouth.

"Speak up girl! You are wasting my time."

Did the sorcerer do something to me so I couldn't share his evil deeds with the world? Ammi turned away, walking out of the kitchen, leaving the pan of caramelized onions on the stove.

I loved the smell of garlic, onions, and crushed pepper frying in butter. Something so simple could make me forget all my ills. She returned, placing the chicken she bought that day from the butcher into a pot of boiling water, and simmering ingredients. All my thoughts were on the results of my mother's labor. All I wanted was to eat as much as I could, so it would be easy to fall asleep, and forget about the day.

After I finished making dough I washed my hands, and left to go see what my sister was doing. I had not seen her enter the house, though it was way past the time she normally got home from school. I looked in my Nani's bedroom first, because that is where Maya usually stayed, waiting for her to come home from the school where she worked.

Nani was usually the last one to leave the school, making her arrive home around 6:00 P.M. every weekday. I went into my grandmother's bedroom, and there was Maya, sitting on the bed, legs curled up against her body-and there was my father, kneeling at her side, caressing her hair. It was a scene I recognized from my past all too well, which instantly through me into a furious fit. That man had come to my bedside, and talked dirty to me at that age. I immediately ran towards the bed, leaping at my father like a wrestler flying through the air.

"You are not going to do this to my sister!" I yelled.

I would stand up for her as I could never do for myself. I rolled my fist into a ball, punching that son of a bitch in the head as hard as I could. After the fifth blow he grabbed my legs, pulling me to the ground. I tried getting up, but to no avail. He was on top of me, pinning me down. When I tried to look to see if my sister was still in the room, he pushed my head back down to the floor. Maya had already leapt out of the bed, pleading to him, yelling, "Stop, please! Stop!"

He was like an octopus with eight hands-one pinning my face to the floor, another grabbing my ass, and everything else he could get his hands on. Then he whispered in my ear, "You will get your turn, Laila, but let me show your little sister some love first."

I did not care what he did to me-the only thing I cared about was Maya not seeing her big sister sodomized. Apparently, my sister saw nothing incriminating. My father finally let go of my head in time for me to see my entire family, mother, grandmother, and brothers, entering the room.

"Nothing going on here," my father said. "I'm just having some fun with my daughters before I leave..."

I looked at my mother and grandmother, expecting them to question this "fun" we were having, but both of them turned around, and walked out of the room while my brothers and sister remained behind. My younger brother, Jawad, ran and dove on top of us. He thought we were wrestling, and jumped on my father's back starting to simulate the moves and techniques. Free from my father's grasp, I immediately grabbed Maya, and pulled her across the room to the door, through the hallway, and into the bathroom.

"Laila, are you okay?" Maya asked, with an innocence I envied. I broke down crying before I took her hand.

"What did you see?" I asked. If he tries anything with Maya, and subjects her to the torture he put me through I will murder him in his sleep whether Allah will forgive me or not. "If he does anything to you, he will pay with his life," I said.

My mother summoned us to the kitchen for dinner. Before my sister could leave I grabbed her hand, and told her to tell me everything our father had said to her. "Don't ever conceal the bad that happens to you," I insisted. "It will eat away at your mind like a cancer."

"Yes, *Baji*-no secrets. But he said nothing," she answered. We left together for the dining area. We all sat around the table in a circle, staring into each others' eyes. That was where all the innocent footsies had begun around my eighth birthday. Because all his attention had been on me, I had thought he loved me so much. He played with me all day long when he was home from work. I had thought my father, Abdulla Hassan, was a great man, a man of Allah, and the perfect father.

Now I see those footsies as the prelude to the sorcerer's ultimate plan to turn me into his personal whore. After he raped me, I always moved my feet at dinner when he tried to touch them with his. If he reached over to touch me, I rose up, scampering away so quickly my mother never had a chance to ask where I was going. My mother and brothers started to look at me like I was weird.

Slowly but surely everything I did become weird and erratic. I never wore anything less than my burqa. I only wore black, and I didn't laugh or play with my siblings anymore. I was always irritable, but now I beat my siblings severely whenever they gave me any trouble. I had become a recluse to my own blood, with no friends, afraid of my own shadow. *I can live with two more weeks of my life like this*, I told myself before I fell asleep.

I woke up feeling refreshed with new, unusual thoughts. How was I going to become normal again? Everything needed to change. I wanted to wait until my father left for good before starting the radical change I concocted in my mind.

The only way I could learn how normal people act was to watch more television. I could not watch TV during the day when my mother would see shows she would not approve of. Two hours of television at night would set me right. I analyzed to see what else I could change about myself to embark on the construction of a new identity. At least I knew love and hate-love for my family, and hate for myself and my father. I needed to start loving myself again.

My peers had started easing up, and did not bother me by yelling out, "Elephant!" as I walked down the hallways. It was a good day. When I arrived home, the only thing I cared about was the exact date my father was leaving. I asked my mother about my father's travel plans, and she told me it would be six days before he left. She noticed how enthusiastic I seemed to see my father go, saying in a very condescending, jaded tone, "You used to love your father so much. What happened?"

This was the platform I had been looking for to air out any dirty laundry, but I still could not bring myself to say it. I sat there in disgust for not being able to speak. The short-lived enthusiasm I had about him leaving vanished.

"Did you feel let down when he went to jail?" I was numb, and could not answer.

"When your father goes to America, he will send for us one by one. We will live there happily. He has friends who will help him to do that. He is doing this for us, so you have to keep respecting him, and love him for what he is doing for us."

A frantic, incendiary feeling came over me as she spoke. "Respect that man? Never!" I exclaimed. A I finished saying, "Never," my face became hot from the slap of my mother's hand.

"This is what I get for protecting this family?" I demanded. "Do you know the sacrifices I have made for you-for my siblings-your children?"

"What are you talking about, stupid girl?" she asked, giggling in a cynical fashion while the words came out of her mouth.

It seemed as though I would be trapped with my secrets forever. Every time I had an opportunity to tell my mother, I could not gather up the courage. I was too afraid of the outcome, because of what had happened to aunty Seema's family.

At least he will be in America, and I will be safe from him. I tried remembering all the things I heard about the United States. I reminded myself that my aunt's independence was directly due to her migration to America. *What is this America about?* I thought. *How can I become independent like her?*

Obsessed with America, I needed to find out everything that happened there. That night, after everyone went to bed, I turned on the nineteen-inch television in the living room, and kept the volume low. It was a small space with a little sofa Nani had since I was three. Sitting down I changed the channel from PTV, the Pakistani local Television Network, to the overseas channels. I recognized the attire of the girls from the porn my father forced me to watch before he was sent to prison.

The first show was full of dark-skinned people, whom I had rarely seen since I'd been back in Pakistan. The last time I saw people so dark was in Saudi Arabia. I always thought they were very beautiful, but the Saudi Arabians believed they existed only to do the menial jobs Saudi citizens didn't want.

My mother, and everyone else, always degraded dark-skinned people-which included my sister and I. Because she felt Maya and I were too dark, my mom gave us a bleaching facial cream, and made sure we used it religiously. I loved people of color, thinking they were exotic looking, and grew to love myself more as I saw the reaction they received from respected and loved people on television.

Next, I flipped to a channel called MTV. Occasionally I switched to a show called "Sex in the City." Vigilant in my secrecy I made sure no one would find me watching these shows. In the late hours I soaked up the music, fashion, and attitude, and fell in love with everything that had to do with the culture of the United States. I also fell in love with the women on "Sex in the City." In my culture it was an abomination to behave like these women, so at the time I guessed this was the reason some Pakistanis called Americans infidels.

After the first night watching about four hours of television, I resolved to fix my ill-fated life. I knew what I had to do to become happy, and I knew how to do it. I needed to get to the free world. I wanted to go to America. After seeing how the women on television free to dress and act the way they wanted, I grew determined to get to America. In order to become happy and free it needed to happen. America was not the land of infidels to me anymore: it was my ticket to freedom.

During the day I had no energy due to sleep deprivation, but it was a small price to pay for what I learned at night. Two nights before my father departed for the U.S. we had dinner with uncle Zafar, his wife, and their children, for whom my family had slaved for when we initially came back from Pakistan.

Of course on the menu were my father's favorite foods. We sat in the living room listening to my uncle and his wife, who had been to America, tell us how morally backwards Americans were, and how my father would surely make a lot of money doing certain types of jobs. My sister and brothers were overjoyed. This was exactly what they wanted to hear. They were already tired of trying to find the virtues of living in poverty. They wanted the life we had back in Saudi Arabia. How did I feel? I was elated he was leaving.

While everyone talked I left, as if I were going to use the bathroom. I was obsessed with what he was bringing with him when he left, so I peeked inside his leather bag of important documents. The ticket said "October 5, 2000, departure time 4:30 P.M." It was the night of October 3, and I counted the minutes until his departure. Uncle Zafar saw the glee in my brothers' and sister's eyes about America, and gave them more details, as if they were calves feeding from their mother's udder.

"The exchange rate is seventy-to-one...I know, because it cost me an arm and a leg to get your father's plane ticket."

"So every American dollar you make will be 70 rupees?"

"Yes."

After listening to them yap about the good and bad of America, my mother and Zafar's wife served dinner. I did not care to eat the meal, because Zafar's wife, who had abused us, had prepared some of the food. I only ate the haleem dish my mother made. I lacked care about anything in that house. I only wanted everyone to leave, so I could pretend to go to bed, and watch American television. That night I would not be bothered by my father, as he and my mother sequestered themselves so they could have some privacy.

As soon as grandmother went to bed around 9:00 P.M., I turned on the television, resuming my love affair with all things American. By the end of the night I wanted nothing more than to buy a ticket to America. I had no clue how this would happen, but I knew I could get my father to do it.

That night I became a calculating and manipulative woman inundated with pride. I had seen enough attitude on the tube to mimic the behavior. I practiced my walk, and within an hour I had it down. Walking through town my sister noticed my new stride. By the time I arrived at the corner one block from our house, Maya whispered, "*Baji*, what is happening to you? Why are you walking that way?"

"Do you like it?"

"A lot, *Baji*," she said, "I like it a lot."

"Well, this is how I am going to walk from now on."

She smiled—understood the ramifications of my new style.

Chapter 10
A New Me

Throughout my time in school, I saw only one girl with the kind of sassy attitude I wanted to emulate. Her name was Nida, and she could teach me the contrasting behavior I needed to fix my inability to save myself. She had lived in America for three years, and spoke proper English. She must have seen these strong women personally, because she sure acted like the ones on television. I waited until lunchtime, and walked right up to her table.

"What do you want?"

"I only want to be your friend." I spoke in a slow, calming, confident voice. She must have seen how sincere I was. She took a bite of her samosa and looked up at me. "You're not one of those lesbian girls, are you?"

"No," I said before she could even finish her sentence. I asked myself that same question many times. I hated the fact that deep down I'd rather the things my father did to me be done by a beautiful woman.

Nida was beautiful. She had long, brown, curly hair, a slim body with big boobs, and skin like smooth, white pearls. Everyone was attracted to her. Pakistani men loved that skin color. The lighter you were, the more attention you attracted. Women wanted to be her.

"Well," she said, eyeing my body up and down, critiquing it, "you are going to have to lose some weight."

My feelings were hurt, but if I wanted to become a better version of myself I would have to take some constructive criticism.

She summoned me to the restroom, where she took me into one of the stalls, and told me to lean over the toilet. It was here she asked my name, and making sure not to sound overeager I told her, "It's Laila."

"Nice to meet you, Laila. You are going to lean over that toilet, and stick your finger down your throat until you throw up." Unquestioningly, impressionably, I followed her directions, and soon was soon regurgitating the meal I had only recently eaten. Nida told me to do this after every meal to become skinny like her.

Other than the acrid taste in my mouth I was content with her plan for me to lose weight. We walked out of the bathroom together. She wasted no time in talking about my bushy eyebrows, and huge hips. She told me she would bring a thread to school the next day to fix my eyebrows. I became beside myself that I had a new friend who knew how to make me pretty.

That evening I eagerly anticipated dinnertime so I could implement Nida's diet plan. Only my sister and father were at home. He must have been waiting for me, because as soon as I entered the door, he told my sister to go buy cigarettes. The nearest store was a quarter-mile away, and he gave Maya some extra money for her to buy candy for her and my brothers.

The minute my sister walked out the door, he grabbed me, literally ripping off my clothes. I tried to run, but he kissed my neck, and everywhere he could get his mouth on. It was only a matter of time before he started humping away like the last time. I started thinking about my new friend, Nida, imagining it was her on top of me.

After the ordeal was over he handed me my school uniform, telling me to put my clothes on before anyone came home. I looked at him to see if he had an ounce of contrition in his eyes, but, as usual, all I saw was unconscionable evil.

I walked into the living room where he sat, satisfyingly smoking a cigarette on the couch in front of the television. I asked him if he loved me, or whether this was just something he did because it felt good. He knelt to his knees, clutching at my legs.

"*Baji*, I love you so much you could not even know. You are the reason why I am going to America, so we can have money to go, and do, whatever we want. Don't let your mom marry you off to any man while I am gone. I love you, Laila. Don't forget that."

I questioned everything I knew. Several times he talked about marrying me off to uncle Zafar's son, Zameer, so why now is he saying I should not marry? Somehow, I loved my father-only not the way he loved me. I loved him before I knew how to say my name, but I did not want to spend the rest of my life with him. I asked how long it would take for him to come back for me. He said it would be about two years until I could go to America, but he would return long before then.

I vowed to remain strong and resolved. I needed to set up a timeline for escaping from that dirty lifestyle once and for all. As he continued to talk my mind was busy planning my escape. My sister re-emerging through the front door snapped me out of my daze. My father lifted himself from the kneeling position, and walked towards Maya, pretending to be concerned with the cigarettes he sent her to buy. Hugging Maya, he told her "Thank you," and asked if she had bought herself candy. It made me sick.

I retired to the bedroom, counting the diamond-shaped holes in the white chalk-tile of the ceiling until I fell asleep.

Until this day I still don't know what happened, but when I awoke, my little sister was rolled up in a ball next to me, crying, rocking her body from side to side. When I asked what was wrong, she told me she was going to miss my father. I didn't believe her. This was the first time I had seen her cry in five years. She had not even wept when he went to jail. I couldn't get her to talk, so I was left to conjecture, and formulate my own thoughts. I thought our father must have done something to her as I lay asleep, but Maya would not confirm my suspicions. I stopped fighting him off when he made his advances, so surely he had no reason to touch my sister.

My mother entered the room asking Maya if she was all right. She told my mother the same story she told me. After that incident I slept about two hours before waking up in the middle of the night with an enormous amount of uneasiness. I was worried my father had molested my sister. I turned on the television, quickly changing it from Pakistani television to my beloved MTV. Soon I was transported to another world, and got caught up in the music videos, beautiful girls, dancing, handsome men, and the rhythm of the music. I loved it! I realized I was not a lesbian. The thoughts of Nida were a coping mechanism my brain deployed to detach from the horrors around me, and my perverted view of life, love, and liberty.

I loved those MTV guys like LL Cool J-so cute and confident. I grew to love bands like Coldplay and Green Day. Bands I never would have known about. Music saved me. It stopped me from counting the seconds incessantly. Music made me focused on getting out of Karachi.

Through music my mind had started to heal. The idea of sacrificing my mind and body for anyone seemed impossible. That night I thought how I wanted my husband to be like one of those guys on MTV. Before falling asleep I imagined how pretty my eyes were going to look after Nida threaded my eyebrows.

I woke up two hours later to the sound of everyone getting ready to leave. My father had to depart early to the airport. Everyone was in tears. Everyone except me. I loomed in the background, on the fringe of two alternate universes, watching the spectacle. There was no pomp or circumstance from me. My resentment was overshadowed by everyone else's grief. Would they grieve if they had known the truth? I could not wait for the torture to stop. I looked on in silence as my father left in an old taxicab, disappearing around the bend of our house, leading to the main road.

Chapter 11
The Calm Before the Storm

My life had taken a significant turn. For the next month, I felt Allah was listening to me by providing Nida as my savior for the time being. She was wild compared to other Pakistani girls. She made me feel like I could do anything. My eyebrows were groomed and well-shaped, my body had become slimmer, and my confidence surged. Thanks to Nida's lessons on how to be a perfect bulimic, I was now just as slim as the rest of the girls in school. She took care of my eyebrows as if they were her own, and while using her thread to make them perfect, she commented time after time how beautiful my eyes were.

Once, Nida was no more than a foot from my face when she told me, "Your eyes are like a perfect half-moon." Her breath on my face became heavier as she stared at me obsessively. This took place under the tree outside where all the girls played during recess. The classrooms were built in a circle around a tall *Neem* tree that created a shady spot on hot, sunny days. I looked forward to those times when she leaned close to me to do my eyebrows.

I knew I didn't love women, because I still looked at the boys who stared at us outside our school every day. They came and sat on their motorbikes, waiting for a glimpse of a girl who was not covered by a burqa. Nida gave me the strength I needed to wake up in the morning and look in the mirror and not see my putrid past looking back at me. Yes, she was a crutch, but my wounded body was healing, and soon she would be an unnecessary accessory.

As I grew slimmer, I started taking care of my hair instead of chopping it off in a wild rage as I tried to purge my thoughts. Nida's compliments grew frequent, along with my respect for her. Others noticed my change, and within two months of my first purging, I had more classmates vying to become my friend than in entire time I was in school.

Sati was just as beautiful as Nida, but not as social. Nida told me how badly Sati had ridiculed me before I started my dramatic makeover, so I ignored her attentions. Also, Sati was a lesbian. At least, that is what Nida told me. A week passed before I finally built up the nerve to ask her how she had formulated that theory. At first Nida said, "She just is." When I continued to confront her, she said Sati had tried to kiss her in the bathroom beside our classroom. Nida swore that she had turned away and run out of the room. She became very frustrated with me, saying, "Give an inch and you take a mile, eh? You want to know everything!"

I apologized immediately. The next day at school while she threaded my eyebrows, Nida explained why she'd grown frustrated so quickly: "I hated when Sati tried to kiss me like a man, and now there is not one day that goes by when I don't think of kissing you."

I stood there, feeling awkward. "I do the same thing, Nida," I admitted. "I daydream of kissing you, too."

I was lying to protect our friendship. I was a habitual liar. Through lying, I learned to protect my family's name and respect in society. Nida started to look at me with lust in her eyes. She obviously knew what she wanted. I thought she was going to kiss me right under the tree, but thanks to Allah, she held back. If she had, and someone had seen, we would have been expelled and whipped until we bled. A few months earlier, a Pakistani girl who was accused of being a lesbian had been stoned to death for leaving her husband and cheating with a woman.

The last hour of class, Nida slid a piece of paper on my desk. The note read, "My dear Laila, I have never felt like this before, and I do not know what to do. I know everything I feel is wrong in the eyes of Allah and Pakistan, but none of that matters. I just want to put my lips on yours. Can we meet in the bathroom after class?"

Those thoughts of kissing became too real for me. As soon as school was over, I dashed out of the class and ran the quarter-mile home. I liked Nida, but the thought of getting intimate with anyone sickened me. I was afraid and wondered if my past had scarred me for life. I thought I had to give Nida what she wanted just to make myself feel capable of being intimate with another human being. I knew then I *had* been scarred for life. At the same time, I felt that my love for Nida was different, and it seemed right. I loved her. At least, I had started to love her.

I decided that evening while I did homework that I would kiss her the next day in the bathroom during break or after school. Compared to all the atrocities I had given into, kissing a girl was nothing, I thought.

As soon as we arrived in class, I gave her note back with an answer: "Meet me in the bathroom during break." She put the note in her uniform pocket, as if I had given her soiled toilet paper. I shrugged it off, thinking she was trying to be discreet.

When the break came, I stood there in the bathroom waiting for her, and my heart paced faster than it had ever before. My asthma was kicking in. I washed my face slowly with cold water and took deep breaths. I waited for what felt like an eternity, but Nida never showed up. I went outside by the tree, but Nida was nowhere to be found. When the bell rang at twelve, she was not back at her desk, either. I became worried, my palms grew sweaty, and I fidgeted with my nails so much that I could hear them crackling.

Had she understood what she was about to do and copped out, or had she realized she really didn't like me as much as she thought and vomited her breakfast when she thought about kissing me?

All the confidence she had instilled in me disappeared in an instant. I went into one of my trances in which I counted everything. I counted the paint-chips on the wall, the teacher's stroke with chalk, the shuffling of the girl's feet in front of me, every single cracked line in the cement floor of our classroom.

I didn't learn anything that day. The bell awakened me from my trance, but I took forever to get up from my seat. Mr. Moeez noticed me still sitting long after everyone had left and walked over to my desk, shooing me out of the classroom as though I were a wild chicken. I walked slowly out of the class and through the front door, looking at the "Pakistani paparazzi" who were there to catch a glimpse of the girls coming out. I must have walked too slowly that day, because one of those guys on a motorbike had the nerve to come up to me on the street. His bike screeched at my feet, and the smell of fuel consumed my good air.

"Good afternoon, young miss," he said. I kept walking, not even looking up at his face. "You need a ride home?"

I stopped and looked at this boy who had the nerve to talk to me. I said nothing at first, while I thought of the most horrible thing to say. "You want to take me on your bike and kidnap me, you piece of excrement?" I blared at him loudly enough for the rest of the men behind us to hear.

A sudden drowning laughter came from them. I said nothing else, as the boy turned his bike around, drove off ahead of me, and disappeared into a plume of dust. I felt bad afterwards. I promised myself that if he ever had the nerve to come up to me again, I would apologize. If he had caught me on a better day, things might have been different.

I kept walking slowly until I felt someone tug on the back of my uniform. It was my sister. She had decided to skip her afternoon tutoring session with the math teacher. Later, when we grew older, she told me he tried to put his hands up her skirt. She never said whether or not he got to the Promised Land. I still don't know what my sister did or did not do. She became a pathological liar, like me, and a great actor. That day she held my hand all the way home, which made me feel good.

When I arrived home, I became weak, quickly fell asleep, and awoke way past dinnertime. There was no dinner in the kitchen, but the dirty dishes remained, and the remnants of *haleem* were in the pots. The smell of my father's favorite food disgusted me. What made it even more terrible was the sick feeling the thought of him elicited in my head. I was happy there was no food to vomit that night. The bulimia had started to take its toll on my breath. I began constantly chewing mint balls to hide the smell. Later on, I decided that I didn't want bad breath for the rest of my life so I later quit being a bulimic.

I happily plopped myself in front of the television. I saw vixens in several videos from rap stars like Eminem, Snoop Dog, and others. I noticed how big most of their assets were. Those women had big hips like mine. I thought to myself that I was in the wrong society. Here I was persecuted day-in and day-out because of the way my body looked, and there in America, these girls were worshipped in videos and songs. I appreciated how confident everyone looked in their big, gold chains and fancy clothes. I soaked up every minute of the culture until 5:00 A.M. and then crawled into bed to get the usual two hours of sleep I squeezed in before dressing for school.

When I walked into class that morning, Nida was already there. She looked different. She had cut off her long, curly, black hair to look like mine. I knew what that meant. She was ashamed of herself, just as I had been many times before. She looked up at me and barely managed to smile. I smiled back, walked over to her desk, and rubbed her shoulder.

"Nida, you've helped me so much, and I love you for that. Please don't be mad at me, and don't be mad at yourself."

I am not sure how I formulated the words to say to her. Nida rose and hugged me the way my little sister usually did—crouching over, holding me around my waist, head against my chest. She finally looked up with tears in her eyes. "Laila, I am so sorry. I felt ashamed. I felt as if I was pushing you to do something you did not want to do. I wanted you to say 'yes' the same day, and when you did not, I went home feeling terrible and quickly swore to myself that this would never happen again." Her voice quivered as she spoke.

I felt consumed by guilt for not having given in to her wishes that same day. It was the type of guilt I felt when my father wanted to touch me in the middle of the day while my mother was in the kitchen. I took Nida's hands from around my waist, as the rest of the classroom was walking in. I did not want to deal with any of my feelings. Nida had just buried herself in the bottomless pit where I buried all the feelings I could no longer handle.

I tried my best to ignore her after that day. I even went so far as to eat lunch under the little tree where the boys ate. Those boys thought I was crazy anyway, so no one paid attention to me. When I saw Nida coming into the yard, I ran to the back of the school and into the bathroom. After about a month, she disappeared from class. I never saw her again.

I was now sixteen. For my birthday, I received a pot full of chicken *biryani* from my mother and a phone call from America. I had not heard from my father for a while. Whenever he called, I heard the phone ring in my Nani's room and pretended I was sleeping just to avoid him. My mother finally realized my deceitful antics and started to wake me up out of my pretend sleep when he called. When I spoke to him, his voice was different, and for once I felt as though he was so far way he could not hurt me. I was wrong. After just five minutes talking about school, he asked if I was behaving myself.

"Staying away from men, *Baji*?"

"Yes."

"Good girl. You're still Daddy's little girl, right *Baji*?"

I knew where the conversation was going by the change in the tone of his voice. My mother was sitting right in front of me while he asked if I was "masturbating and thinking of the sex we had." I became so sick, I handed my mother the phone and ran to the bathroom, where I threw up in the sink. My nausea was so severe that I had to sit on the floor to keep from falling over.

I was sick! It was a combination of complete memory recall and the fact that this man was sitting where he was, thinking about what he did to me, waiting to come back to do more damage. It took about an hour to calm down and go back to my bed. I knew that if I did not pretend to fall asleep, my mother would interrogate me to find out why I had run out of the room. As soon as she stopped talking to the sorcerer, I put the sheet over my head and pretended to be asleep.

Chapter 12
Stick To The Plan

I stayed up all night thinking about how not to answer the phone when my father called. The memories I had blocked for a year were all coming back, torturing me like a captured prisoner. When everyone was asleep, I finally escaped the misery of my thoughts. I slipped into the living area, turned on the television, and quickly forgot every thought when the music videos played on VH1 and MTV channels.

Let's stick to the plan, Laila, I told myself. America, hip-hop music, and lifestyle will only cost you a few sleazy phone calls pretending to want that nasty bastard. I listened for my mother to call my brothers to answer the phone. Once they said, "*Allah Hafiz* (goodbye)," it was my turn to get on the phone and tell him I missed him so much. I couldn't. The first sound of his voice made all my strength evaporate, and all I could say was, "Yes, a-hah, a-hah," to all his questions.

"Do you miss me? I miss you, *Baji*," and, "Are you playing with yourself and thinking about me? Don't put anything inside."

"Yes."

Getting through those questions without throwing up or feeling nauseated was good enough for me. I started to talk to him only when my dream came to the forefront of my thoughts.

"When are you coming? We all miss you. When are you going to take us?"

I made sure to say "us," so I wouldn't seem selfish to my mother and brothers, who sat only a couple of feet from me.

My father was silent for ten seconds. Then he said, "I did not know you guys would want to come here, so I did not plan to file for any visa. A visa for you all could take years," he added. That man was so conniving! Before he left us, he had said his plan was to take me there.

"But I will see you when December comes around," he said. It was only February.

I put the phone down, feeling no hope of ever getting to where I wanted to be. I stopped paying attention to what he said and thought of the images of girls dancing and having fun driving to the nearest club with their friends. I handed the phone back to my mother and went to the bathroom. Looking at my face, I started to mark it with the *kajal* (Indian eye blackener) that rested on the sink. After a while, I could no longer see my face, which made me happy. I could not see the face of the person who pretended to like that man.

I quickly snapped out of my pity party and decided I really had to do something to make this man hurry the process of taking me to the United States. As long as I was there in Karachi, I would be subjected to him when he came to visit. If my mother chose a husband for me, my father would disapprove so he could have me for himself. I thought for a while in the bathroom until I heard my sister knock.

I thought about running away, but of course the negative images painted by my mother about girls getting raped and murdered was my main deterrent. In Pakistan, I would end up in the sex-slave trade like the girls I saw on the corner near the market.

Most of them had run away from their homes or had come over the border from Afghanistan, where they had sometimes been sold by their own parents. The only choice I had was to be patient and wait for the same person from whom I was running to rescue me. I had to use him the way he had used me for all those years.

I had to be very persuasive when he called, so he would think I would be his personal sex slave when I arrived in America. I needed to make him believe I could be an asset to him there. Then I could run away when the time was right.

I went to the store and bought phone cards with money I stole from my mother's purse and started to call him when everyone was asleep. I phoned him for the first time about a week after my birthday. I knew he would be elated that I had called him. He went on and on about how proud he was of me, saying, "I knew one day you would want me just as much as I want you." He thought all the years of him brainwashing me had finally paid off and that I finally needed him. I played along as if I were Carey Bradshaw from "*Sex in the City.*"

"I miss you so much. I have not forgotten a single thing we did together."

He sounded as if every word made him high on *hashish*, moaning and calling my name as he masturbated, finishing up in minutes. I knew right then and there that I was going to be in the United States faster than anyone else in my family.

I started complaining to him how I missed him, how the men outside school had started to stare at me more, and how Ammi continuously talked about marrying me off to the guys who lived in the rich neighborhoods. All of this made him furious. It was then he told me of a way to get me to the U.S quickly.

"I can find an American and marry her, and that would make me an American citizen in no time. Then I could file for you and get you here quickly," he said.

I became ill when the phone call finished. I felt as if someone had pummeled me with a bat. Pretending to like him had drained all the energy from me. I was elated, though, because I knew I was on my way to freedom.

The conversation was the same three nights later. It ended with him telling me he knew whom he was going to "fake marry" to get his citizenship. I went to bed that night begging Allah to give me the strength to take control of my life. I soaked up every scene on American television at night in preparation for life in the U.S.

I started to do well in school because I also had to convince my mother to let me go to the States. I knew she would tell my father when he called that I would be an asset to him in America. It was all a part of the plan, and I carried it out as if I were possessed. I was driven by the evil that had been done to me. I did not care about staying in Pakistan and rotting like my cousin Abeera had.

One day I will have to tell this secret to Ammi, but I'll be damned if it will destroy my life, I reminded myself almost daily.

With each day, I became stronger, although I still felt nauseated when I thought about my past. Somehow, my father had his marriage legally annulled in Pakistan within two months of my telling him I wanted to go to America. I was infuriated that he would do this to my mother just to facilitate his sick dream of having himself and me together.

I will surely stab him to death when I get to America and plead insanity for the years of abuse, I thought. I had learned about the insanity plea from *"Law and Order,"* an American show with intricate details about the American judicial system. I knew about his marriage to the woman about five months before my mother found out. I lived with fear in my heart for those five months; I knew the news was going to devastate her.

I started to prepare for the day when I would have to start taking care of my family as I had after Ammi gave birth to Maya instead of the son she wanted, and after my father went to jail. The day after I found out my father had annulled his marriage, I felt guilty when my mother made me breakfast. I knew what had been done to her in the past, and things were not going to improve. If Ammi's mother had chosen someone better as her husband, I would be different, my mother would be different, and we wouldn't have suffered so badly.

As she smiled and told me to do well in school, I looked at her for the first time in a long time.

"Ammi, we are going to be okay," I promised, "You know I love you, right? And all of us love you, right? So be happy regardless of what happens."

I said it in the softest possible way with all the sincerity my cold heart could muster. Yes, my heart had become cold. I had to be cold in order to survive the trauma I endured.

Chapter 13
The Blur Days

Attending school became a tedious task that I performed only to avoid being beaten by my mother. The guy on the motorbike whom I had embarrassed months earlier confronted me one day after school finished. He rode his bike up to me after I had walked about half a mile from school. I thought he was going to pull out his gun and shoot me for embarrassing him in front of his friends. At first I was scared, but seconds later, I was at peace with myself after flashbacks erupted in my mind of all the filthy things my own father had done to me. I became happy that this guy could possibly kill me.

He got off his bike, stood in front of me, and reached into the pocket of the bag hung over his shoulder. Instead of a gun, he pulled out a rose with a letter tied to it! He handed it to me, mounted his bike, and rode off, once again leaving a trail of dust as if he were a movie villain. I looked around to see if anyone I knew had seen this transaction. Except a girl from a different grade walking behind me, there was no one around. I ripped off the note, smelled the rose, and threw it in the alley behind the corner store at the end of the block where my house stood.

I dared not let my mother see the rose; she would think I was out there giving my virginity away, which was punishable by death in some rural areas of Pakistan. In Karachi, a swift beating and probable banishment from the girl's home would be warranted. I scurried into the house and read the note:

Thank you very much for disrespecting me in front of my friends. I watch you every day coming from school, amazed at how beautiful you are, and this is the thanks I get? I want you to apologize to me by having a Pepsi with me downtown at the mall tomorrow.

I was impressed by the gesture and immediately decided I would go with him on his bike after school the next day. I had nothing to lose. What was the worst that could happen? He could have maimed me, killed me, and put me in a ditch; it really hadn't mattered to me at the time. I did not fear that boy. Fear comes when you have something or someone to live for, and I had neither.

I wasn't even sure what he looked like when I thought about him that night. I had seen him twice: first when I was angry and the second time when I was scared to be seen talking with him. I told myself that tomorrow I would take a good look at him. The more I thought about it, the more I realized that no matter what he looked like, he did not stand a chance with me.

I wanted someone who respected women and treated them like goddesses, not like property. I thought all men in Pakistan and Saudi Arabia wanted to control their women. Furthermore, I did not have time to think about this fool. I had to focus on getting good grades and getting myself out of Pakistan. Ammi came into the room that night, telling me that my father had called, and she had told him how well I was doing in school.

Just as I planned it, I thought. I purchased another calling card from the money my mother had saved for a rainy day in the pillows she slept with. I called my father after everyone was asleep. This time around, he did not use that sleazy tone of his. Instead, he started to talk in a very business-like voice.

"I heard you're doing well in school over there. I will try my best to get you here. I always thought I would have to wait for my sons to grow up to help me build and grow my family, but since you are the firstborn, and you are doing so well and trying so hard, I am going to bring you here quickly so you can help me."

"Another way to use Laila," I thought.

"Yes, Dad, I will come there and go to university. I'll get a graduate degree and take care of you and all our family," I answered, with great enthusiasm in my voice.

"Okay, I'm getting married in two weeks to this lady I met through my boss here," he promised. "She is White and fat, but I can use her to get you here as quickly as possible then get rid of her."

It was just like him—ready to ruin another person's life for selfish reasons. I knew it was wrong but because he did what I asked it gave me a sense of power over him. Then I realized he had somehow convinced himself I was going to be loyal to him just as his wife had been for sixteen years.

Why *was* she so loyal, anyway? I would never become one of those Muslim women who live for their husbands and not for themselves. I decided that the next sixteen years of my life were going to be dictated by me, Laila! I was going to do what I wanted to do and become who I wanted to be! That piece of dog poop was not going to make me a debilitated zombie like my mother. I was going to live like an independent queen in New York, like those girls on "*Sex in the City.*"

I immediately switched on the television to feed my addiction to the American lifestyle. The movie *New Jack City* was on, and enjoyed every minute of it. Nino Brown was my new American idol. He did not have a beard, his skin was dark, chocolate brown, and he was a rich outlaw. I was an addict for all things American, and that night I had my fix. I sat on the floor of Nani's home, convinced I was no longer a victim. I fell asleep in a cocoon filled with pride.

Two nights later, when my father called, he spoke only to Ammi and told her his plan to bring me to the United States. My mother looked at me with mild perplexity while she listened to him talk about why he wanted me in the United States. He told her that I would become a huge asset to the family if I were there. In Pakistan, the school faculty chooses what you study in college based on your high school performance. I did well in math and science, so they had chosen engineering as my line of study.

My father told Ammi I would excel in an American university and end up making more money than he would ever make working menial jobs for his Pakistani friends. I don't think she bought it, because when she finished talking, Ammi quickly went into my Nani's room and flung the phone to me before scurrying off.

I said, "Hello." He must have thought it was my mother and continued to talk. I let him. I wanted to hear the excrement that he fed my mother to make her buy his explanations.

"I can send for Laila first, and then I will send for the rest of the family a couple of years after she finishes college," he insisted.

His excitement made me sad because I knew my mother didn't know this man was going to betray her by marrying someone else. She didn't realize he was actively trying to bring me to the U.S. for himself. He wanted to steal the rest of my life away. He planned to take me to America to be his personal sex slave and to work and take care of him and his family financially.

I became overwhelmed listening to him and started to yell into the phone. "How are you going to have two wives in America? You are never going to pull this off. I am never going to come there and work for you," I said in the meanest sounding voice I could muster. I hung up the phone, not knowing what had come over me, and started to think about my plan.

That day I accepted that my mother would become collateral damage — the price I had to pay for my freedom. I realized I could not let my true feelings show again. I needed to become as selfish as the sorcerer, or else I would surely fail and be stuck in this nasty lifestyle. I went directly to comfort my mother.

"What's bothering you, Ammi?" I asked.

"I wanted a better life for you, but I wanted to be there with you all the way. Your father wants you to go to America and help him. He always said he would never have his children grow in America and become like American children. I don't want you to be like that either," she said in a soft voice.

"Don't worry, Ammi. If I get there, I will work and send you money to buy your own home. I won't let you down, Mom. I'm not going to become like those American children."

I had become adept at lying; it was easy to sit there and lie to my mother that everything was going to be okay. My father never did buy my mother a house. He had made millions of rupees over the years, buying cars for his brothers and starting them out with businesses. My mother always came last. Helping her would be the first thing I would do when I got to America. I prayed that night for Allah to keep my father alive and well so I could get out of this situation. There we were, all five of us sleeping in my grandmother's spare room, and all the sorcerer could think about was when he was going to get a chance to steal more of my dignity.

I hugged my mother that night as I'd never hugged her before. I wanted her to feel me. I think she did. She hugged me back for what felt like an eternity. I started to tell her how I felt about my father—just the surface stuff, of course. I was trying to prepare for the tsunami ahead by hitting her with small waves.

"He is a selfish user, Ammi. He does not care about you as much as you think he does."

I wanted to tell her myself what he had planned to do, but before I could, I felt a slap on my face so hard my ears rang immediately.

"Don't talk about your father like that! He is the only provider in this family, and until you can walk in those shoes, you will respect him."

What Ammi did had no effect on me whatsoever. I felt nothing. If she had known the truth, she might have behaved differently. I wanted to use my knowledge about what my father was about to do to her in the upcoming months as revenge, but instead, I used it as fuel to walk out of the room thinking Allah had taken his revenge on her already, so I didn't have to do anything to Ammi.

I went directly to the bathroom, where I rubbed my ear to regain my hearing. It took about five minutes for the ringing to stop and another ten for my hearing to come back. I felt no pain, though there were marks on my face. I sat there looking at the small welts closely in the mirror while my heart cried out for forgiveness from my mother. Ammi had no idea what she had done. If she knew how much I loved her. I loved her one hundred times more than I loved the sorcerer she tried to defend. Her anger had not hurt me physically, but it had done so mentally.

I never tried to console her after she slapped me. Whatever happened had happened because of what my father had done. I loved her, but not more than my own life. I had become a soldier trying to stay alive in a war, and there were going to be casualties.

I didn't cry that night in the bathroom. I knew then that I was becoming stronger and battle-ready. I waited until my mother was asleep to steal three rupees from her bag to buy a phone card the next day, but she had no change, so I stole from my grandmother for the first time. Things I thought I couldn't do before now became effortless tasks. I waited until I heard Nani snoring before I crawled into the room with a cigarette lighter my father had left behind. I lit the light sporadically to find my way to the stash of money she kept underneath her Quran. I took seventy rupees out of the hundreds that were there.

I turned off the lighter after I tucked the money in my mouth and crawled back out of the room. I sat in the living room in the dark with the TV on, thinking about what I was going to say to my father to make up for hanging up the phone on him. It was easy; all I had to do was talk dirty to him the way I had seen it done in the movies. As I flipped through the channels, I couldn't help but think about who I was becoming.

I wondered what weird behavior I would exhibit as a result of the new perversion to which I was about to subject my brain. I then thought to myself, maybe when I get to America, there will be a drug I can take to help me forget and stop these nightmares. Yes, I constantly had nightmares and daydreams of my father raping me. I dreamt I was being chased by four men, who caught me, tied me up, and raped me. Those were the normal dreams. In the really bad ones, I was getting married to my father and could not wake up to stop the wedding.

The new phone calls I subjected myself to did nothing to help me heal. I became more and more detached from myself, or who I thought I was. I got off on the fact that I was more in control than anyone else in my family. The reality was that I was becoming more out of control mentally. As I listened to my father beg me to talk dirty to him, I enjoyed the power I felt over him.

Every conversation with that man reminded me what a filthy human being I had become. The same thing happened when I dreamt of the things he had done to me. I was sick, and I knew it. I had no choice but to become a different person. The woman who was aroused by those things was different from the one who wanted to free herself from the disease that was eating her alive. I started to realize I was developing a split personality.

After a night on the phone, I went to school the next day feeling proud. Nothing bothered me. I took care of my brothers and watched them as they grew. I hate to say it, but the resentment I felt as a child toward my brothers did not disappear so easily. My heart was free from any loathsome feelings for them, but I never forgot that they received my mother's love freely, while I had to work for it.

My brothers respected me most of the time, as I demanded it from them; anything less and I became ruthless towards them. My brothers excelled in school, probably in part because of the high-protein diet my mother sacrificed to provide for them. The person I was during the day praised them and loved them, but at night, they were part of my motivation to get out of Pakistan.

In the next phone call, my father asked if I wanted him, and I told him, "So bad that I've started to dream about you every day." My words excited him, and within minutes, he was done. Then he started to talk seriously with me.

"You can't let your mother think anything is wrong, or she will never put you on a plane to America. Keep your thoughts to your damn self and don't be telling your little sister either, because she can't keep her mouth shut."

He sounded upset. I thought to myself, the nerve of this guy. This man had no idea how close I came several times to telling my mother everything. I said nothing. He kept talking, but I heard nothing as I daydreamed about my freedom.

"Yes, Dad, I won't let it happen," I said finally.

He told me he loved me and hung up. I sat there with the phone in my hand for about five minutes before I could hang it up. I was numb; I could not help my thoughts. I started to wonder if what I did was worth it.

I finally hung the phone up, arose, and turned the television volume up. Speaking in English, the newscaster from the satellite channel said something was no accident that it had to be a terrorist attack. As he spoke, I saw a plane flying into a building beside another that was already on fire. This was no movie, but a horror show was on the screen that night. I saw people leaping to their deaths while others ran for their lives. I had seen the Taliban cut people's heads off in Afghanistan, but this was like nothing I'd seen before.

At the time, my father was in Seattle, but somehow I knew the attack on America would affect my plans. I listened to the news until morning. I knew this attack was the work of the *jihadists* I had seen in mosques and in my homes in Saudi Arabia and Pakistan. The buildings finally came crashing down, taking my dreams of escaping the grasp of that madman with them.

When I awoke, I was so depressed and weak that I could not attend school. I sat in my house and heard the occasional AK-47 shots go off with "death to America" following behind. I took it personally; I felt as though they were celebrating my death. I did not eat that night, did not watch television, did not brush my teeth or bathe my skin.

The next morning I dragged myself out of bed and went directly to the television. The Pakistani channel aired the attack on New York City, the home of my idols. I felt bad for those innocent people who lost their lives for no apparent reason. I understood they were infidels, but *I* had experienced a Muslim's atrocities, and nothing ever happened to *him*.

I stopped praying that night. I could not believe that Allah would allow this to happen to innocent people. He had allowed that man to pillage my soul for years and did nothing about it. My faith in Allah was shaken. I watched an hour of news, then returned to bed. When my mother woke me to go to school, I told her how ill I was until she left me alone.

I felt as though I were in a coma because every time I woke up, I felt hopeless and went right back to sleep. I had no strength left in me. I had no visa, no America to look forward to anymore. Several times, my mother came to offer me food, but I never budged. I slept all day until 10:00 P.M. that night and then turned on the television to see something besides the terror attack. I watched two episodes of "The Simpsons" before the phone rang. It was my father, of course.

I answered in such a depressed voice that he immediately asked me, "What is the matter with you?"

I did not respond. He mentioned that it might take longer for me to go to America after what had happened, but he assured me that, "One way or the other, I am going to get you here."

I thought for a second. Did this man realize what was happening? "It is going to take years. Have you seen what those *jihadists* did to those buildings, to America?"

"That is just temporary," he said. "I am getting married to a citizen of the United States." He said it in such a boastful way, it gave me hope my dreams might still come true.

"I am getting married next week. You will be here by the end of the year. I already told her about you and your siblings. She wants to help you come here and be a daughter to her."

I immediately thought to myself that this lady must be broken mentally to want to marry a married man and have someone she has never seen as her daughter.

He had found someone to use to get what he wanted, just as he had done to everyone who entered his life. Because of him, my mother had lost all her family. He had kept borrowing money from them and not paying them back. He assured me that he would have a visa for me within one year. I listened as he boasted how much money the woman had and how high her salary was. Before ever speaking with her on the phone, I knew more about her than I knew of my own mother. She was white and worked at a hospital. She was fat and lived alone. My father babbled on and on for about an hour, and then, of course, he slowly slipped into his sex voice. I could not bring myself to play phone games that night and quickly told him that mother was waking and I had to hang up.

As soon as I got off the phone, I realized how hungry I was. I dragged myself to the kitchen and went into the fridge. There they were—my last three meals neatly packed into to the back of the fridge behind the vegetables. I thought about how much my mom loved me while I ate rice and chicken curry with my fingers. She was by no means perfect, but I knew she loved me. Ammi had her ways to make me feel special sometimes. I loved her, too. I thought maybe when I became successful I would tell her what had happened to me and bring her to live with me in America. It was going to be a tough task, as I knew how faithful and loyal she was to my father.

By the time I finished eating and had started to wash the plates, my mother walked into the kitchen, startled to see me awake. She literally ran me out of the room, warning me that I *would* attend school tomorrow, even if she had to drag me there by my hair. The clock on the little table with my mother's Quran said 1:45 A.M. In the bedroom, I prepared my spot on the ground beside Maya and covered myself with our shared blanket.

As usual, she woke up and growled at me as if I were a dog stealing her bone. She tugged at the blanket with such force that I wondered how someone who weighed less than seventy pounds could be that strong. Once again, I was forced to take what little cover she left for me. I covered my feet and then covered the top of my body with the clothes I had worn the day before.

I fell asleep that night with no peace in my heart. I thought to myself that whoever that lady was, she would not find out what an evil man my father was before the time it took for me to get to America. I could not sleep, tormented by the thoughts of how much garbage I would have to put up with in order to escape my own father. I must have fallen asleep around 5:00 A.M. after my brain couldn't take the truth about my life anymore.

Chapter 14
The Price of Freedom

For the next five months, I was like the girl from the *Girl Six* movie I had watched on television. The star played a girl who worked for one of the sex-chat outfits and became addicted to her work. I related very well to her. A month before my five-month stint as a phone sex operator for the sorcerer, I started thinking about what it would be like to have someone love me. Those thoughts started one night while I watched *My Girl*, a film about two children who fell in love and stayed in love as adults.

After the film finished around 1:00 A.M., I sat and thought about real love and what it would be like to have it from a good boy. For the second time in my life, I felt I could love someone who was not a member of my family, but those thoughts were short-lived. A sudden rush of anxious thoughts mixed with questions in my mind.

Who would want someone like me? I would have to hide my past. Wouldn't he know that I was not a virgin? Wouldn't he realize I was "not all there mentally" after having a couple of conversations? Who could love me? Who could take care of me? Allah forbid my mother gets a chance to marry me off to one of these Pakistani men. He probably would dump me back on my mother once he found out I was a lunatic and not a virgin!

I regressed into the mental state I had been in before I met Nida. Reality set in; I was tainted goods, not worth having. I cried myself to sleep in front of the television. The next morning, I went to school with no desire to live. I thought about how to kill myself while I walked, slowly counting the pebbles on the dirt road that led to my school.

Fifty-five ... Maybe I can slit my wrists behind the big rock behind my house, but that would be too painful...Fifty-nine...I could take those pills that grandmother had for headaches, killing all the pain

I've endured...Sixty-three...Maybe I'd just step in front one those W41 buses that are always racing each other, which killed my cousin.

As the school came into view, I quickly turned around, heading right back home. Just the thought of standing in the long assembly line in the hot sun — itching to move, but fearing the humiliation of being brought on the stage and caned with the big ruler — made me even more miserable. I knew I'd be alone at home. Usually, my mother went to the market after we left for school to buy meat for her little princes. She took such good care of them.

As I walked through the steel gates of my home, with the concrete walls on both sides, I was appalled. It was my mother! I was too early. She was just leaving, closing the huge steel door. We lived in the upstairs apartment, while another family lived on the lower level. When Ammi caught a glimpse of me behind the guava tree, she stopped walking instantly. She was as surprised as I was, yelling my name in that slow, rising voice that signaled trouble for me.

"Not another day! You left school again! Don't you want anything from this life? I can't even marry you off because you're so fat. You'd better get an education so you can fend for yourself."

I did not say a word as I walked past her, entering the steel door. It was then that she unleashed her anger towards me. She hit me with the jute bag in which she carried her food. I ran inside the house to escape the barrage of blows that she was bestowing upon my head. I ran into the kitchen, which was a big mistake. There were too many objects that could be used as weapons there, too many projectiles. Anything in the reach of her hands was a weapon. The pots sitting on the stove from the night before crashed into my head, leaving me stumbling to the ground.

Several times she hit me in the head with a pot, and when it didn't hit my head, it banged against my hands, which I used to protect my head. While hitting me, she kept yelling randomly, as if she was telling me why she was pummeling me which such force.

"All the sacrifices I have made to have you children. If it was not for having you, I would have run away from your father, and now you're missing school when you feel like it!" At first I paid attention only to where the pots crashed on my head, but then, when the line about the sacrifices came out of her mouth, I became infuriated.

"Sacrifice?!" I kept yelling the same word. The yelling scared her so much, she immediately stopped hitting me. I yelled some more. "Sacrifice? What do you know about sacrifice? I am the one who's been making all the sacrifices in this family. I don't even remember being a child! I don't remember you being a mother to me. I cook and clean. I took care of my sister because you were depressed all the time when you only had girls instead of boys. Don't tell me about sacrifice!"

My mother started to cry, saying, "I never did that to you." I ignored her and walked out of the kitchen and into my grandmother's bedroom.

When I crawled into the bed, I started to realize the damage my mother had done. My right hand was swollen all over, and my head ached from front to back. I threw myself face-first into the bed, hoping the sheets would suffocate me and take me from this cruel world. As I lay there in pain, I made the decision to end my poor excuse for a life.

With that decision, came an overwhelming sense of peace, numbing the pain that riddled my body. I reached over to the bedside table where my grandmother kept her pills, grabbed the bottle out of the drawer, and swallowed the contents until I couldn't swallow anymore. All I can remember before I passed out was that my mouth tasted extremely bitter. I started to daydream of all the sweet candies and chocolates father had bought for me in Mecca.

I did not die. I awoke to my grandmother standing over me, demanding to use her bed. I was helpless, shameful, and angry when I realized I was not dead. What the hell was in those pills anyway? I arose up and headed to the bathroom, where I immediately sat on the toilet. I spent the night there with extreme diarrhea. All night I was sick. Not only had I not died, but now I felt the pain in my hands, head, and buttocks. I wondered if Ammi even knew what she'd pushed me to do. I probably would have tried to end my life anyway. Yes, I wanted to kill myself, but I had never acted on my ideas and physically tried to kill myself before that day. I was too afraid of the punishment my grandmother had quoted from the Quran: "If you kill yourself, you will burn in hell for eternity."

My sister woke up that night around 2:00 A.M., which was usual for her. As soon as she saw me crouching down in the bathroom, she asked if I was okay. I guess I was waiting for someone to come and find me in that state because I quickly told her what had transpired earlier.

"Ammi wants to tell me about sacrifice. Do you how much sacrifice I have made for this family, Maya? Do you know? She beat me yesterday because I left school early and she caught me." I was still angry about my mother's "sacrifice" comment.

"So she beat you and made your stomach hurt?" Maya asked.

I answered, "No! That's from the bottle of pills I swallowed from grandmother's drawer. I was trying to kill myself, but they only put me to sleep, and now

I have this bad bellyache." When Maya's face lit up with concern, I realized quickly I had said words that were forbidden to her ears.

"Why are you trying to kill yourself, *Baji*? Why would you want to do that to yourself — and me? Why would you want to leave me here by myself?"

I felt guilty! I felt compelled to give her the reason why I would attempt such a selfish act. "Close the door," I said.

"The disgusting son of a bitch has been raping me, treating me like his whore."

I didn't have to say who the culprit was. Maya started to cry uncontrollably. As she hugged me, she soaked my stomach with tears because she was so short. Seeing her cry also made me cry. We sat there sobbing together for about an hour. After I wiped her tears, she started to calm down.

Maya could not stop talking. "That man is dead to me now!" she yelled. "He tried to take me out of the bedroom in Mecca when I was sleeping with Mom," she continued. "I told him I was going to start yelling, which made him let me go. I just knew there something going on, but when I asked, you said nothing was wrong. You should not be trying to kill yourself, but you should be trying to kill him! I will kill him for you when he comes back here. He is a disgusting, wild beast who needs to be slaughtered. Don't try to kill yourself, Laila. I need you around! I thought you had gone crazy, but now I know why you act that way. I love you, *Baji*. Please don't forget that. We will get through this."

While she spoke, I realized I had not been as good to her lately as I had been in Mecca. I felt terrible for her. I remembered how much I loved her. I asked myself why she hadn't told me what happened the night that he tried to take her out of the room. I would have surely castrated him, making certain he did not repeat the despicable acts with my little sister. I became filled with hate and didn't feel the pain from the beating anymore. From that evening and up until this day, I always tell my sister everything.

We stayed up the entire night. It was a good thing for me, a time to purge the filth that had clogged up my head. With each incident I shared with Maya, I felt lighter. I shared all my experiences from the time I was eight years old. She listened with a look of permanent disgust on her face. After I was done, my little sister was speechless for the first time.

Maya hung her head, looking at the bathroom floor, then looked up and said, "How does Allah allow this man to live? Why is he not dead? We should kill him when he comes back."

As she spoke of murdering my father, I realized my sister was stronger than I was. While I marveled at her strength, I realized how weak I was. Why had I not yelled out in Mecca? Why had I not threatened to scream? Seconds after that thought occurred to me, my mother banged on the bathroom door and beckoned for us to come for breakfast.

"You girls getting ready for school?" she yelled.

Maya answered "Yes, Mom." We quickly washed our faces, headed out of the bathroom, and went to the closet where our clothes hung.

I ate nothing before heading out to school. Mother took notice, and on my way out through the door, she called out to me. "My daughter, please eat something. Don't be upset at me, please. I am so sorry for what I did. I took out my anger on you. I just want you to do well in school so you won't have to put up with the things I have had to bear. Please come back and eat something."

This was a change from her telling me not to eat because I was too big to get a husband! I saw tears coming down her cheeks, which made me return inside and eat the *roti* and milk she had made for me. I had mixed feelings for my mother that morning, but I did not want to see her cry. I quickly ate the food and told her goodbye.

While walking to school, I realized why she had been against me marrying my father's cousin, who was five years older than me. My aunt and her husband had come to our house to ask for him to marry me. My mother vehemently turned them down. My grandmother told them, "Don't ever come to my doorstep if you try to marry that filthy creature, and if I die, don't ever come to my graveside either... filthy creature."

Ammi never gave them a reason why. She just quietly ushered them out the front door. It was weird, because I had thought surely she would have packed our belongings and begged the first man who walked through the door to take me or my sister. I thought she turned down the cousin because he was uneducated. I realized now that she was trying to protect me from what she had been through. Marrying the wrong man had been her downfall. For the first time in a long time, I felt my mother cared about me.

I arrived at school and tried to take notes during the lecture, but it was too painful. The blows from pots the day before had made me sore and uncomfortable. The pain in my hand radiated with a sensation of thousands of sewing pins sticking me at the same time. I tried to listen to my teacher, but I could not think because I was now counting every letter of every word that came out of his mouth. I counted every character like a laptop in Microsoft Word mode. I tried to think of what my mother had done earlier, but I couldn't. The counting intruded on every thought I had. I couldn't stop the machine in my head that was now actively taking over my brain.

Anxiety crept in when I realized I had lost control of my mind. I needed to reboot my brain. End task! Program not responding!

I quickly ran to the bathroom, which was usually empty during class time. I pushed the door with both hands, headed for the stalls, and grabbed the heavy wooden door that swung freely from side to side. I grasped the door tightly, placed myself inside the stall, and slammed the door dead into my forehead. Staggering back, barely able to stand up, my feet guided me to the toilet seat, where I sat for a minute, holding my head. It worked. The crash caused my brain to freeze enough to free me of my counting compulsion. I walked back to class, where I sat for another hour. I did not count another letter. It was like I wasn't even there.

When the bell rang at the end of the school day, I arose from my seat and walked slowly to the door. Turning the corner into traffic made my head feel as if it grew smaller, then bigger, every other second. I slowly walked out the front door and went through the school gate.

"Get me home, Allah. Don't let me pass out on the street," I prayed. I was nauseated from not eating all day, and the combination of the aches all over made me feel my body would give out at any minute. The bike boy was there. I noticed him among the other thirty to forty guys on bikes. He must have seen me walking gingerly, because he sped up, leaving me startled by the bike noise.

"Are you okay, young miss?" I did not answer him. "Young miss, I know you don't like me, but it is obvious you're not feeling right, eh."

I turned to the side to look at his face, but I could not see any of his features, only a distorted double figure. I had no choice but to speak to save myself.

"I'm not feeling good." He jumped off his bike as if the thing were on fire and ran towards me.

"Come, come now. Let me take you home before you pass out on the street. I will take you to your door," he said, his voice quivering. I had no choice but to trust the stranger who was now obviously actively stalking me.

"Okay, just take me home, no place else," I said in a stern voice with all the strength I had left.

He jumped back on his red bike with the white fenders just as fast as he had jumped off. "Come, I'll take you home."

I mounted the bike, gingerly holding onto his shoulder. It was the closest I had ever been to a man who was not a member of my family.

"Put your hands around my waist, hold tight, and don't fall," he said. Off we went, kicking up dust from the dirt road. He didn't utter a word all the way home. I enjoyed the breeze hitting my face as if I were standing in front of the little fan we had at home to ward off heat stroke on 105-degree days.

"Turn here, and leave me at the corner. Thank you," I said. I was weak, but I would rather fall on the street-side than let someone from my house or my neighbors see me getting off a bike from school.

I walked about four steps before he said, "The least you can do is tell me your name, young miss."
I walked three more steps, turned, and said, "It's Young Miss." He smiled, tilting his head to the side. "Laila. What's yours?" I asked, smiling back.

"It's Farooq. See you tomorrow, Laila."
I said nothing and walked away. He drove past me and then turned his bike around and waved at me.

I made it home to see my mother sitting on the front porch, waiting for me to arrive. She rose up as soon as I arrived at the gate.

"Laila, I made curry chicken for you," she said. Ammi put her hand around me as soon as my feet touched the porch, guiding me inside the house.

"Come, sit, eat," she said. My mother didn't have to apologize that day. An aura of guilt filled that kitchen like the strong Indian spices she used. For the first time, she treated me like one of her princes. My little brothers got that attention every day, so what did one night of being treated like nobility mean to me? I realized how much I missed being pampered. The last time I had that kind of attention was close to ten years earlier when my father treated me like his princess.

I blamed myself that day for becoming a different person and alienating my mother. I had been abusive to her, too. I had made her life harder by talking back to her, slapping my siblings around, and attacking any of my extended family for something I remotely didn't like.

After Ammi fed me and told me she loved me, I lay in my grandmother's bedroom, where mother followed me, as if she were my humble servant. Ammi helped me take my clothes off and put on one of the two dresses I wore in the house. I lay on the bed while she fetched the hair brush from our bedroom. Ammi sat at the side of the bed and told me to put my head in her lap, where she slowly brushed my hair and talked to me about her past. She told me how my father's father had treated her like a slave and how it affected her.

"I was never there for you Laila. I was so depressed by what they did to me."

This was the first time she had ever spoken about her seven years of depression. I felt overwhelmed by the sea of emotions the past twenty-four hours had brought. I closed my eyes and tried not to think about what my mother was saying. I fell asleep at peace. For the first time in years, I slept uninterrupted through the night.

I woke up the next morning feeling free. I did not contemplate killing myself that day. I went to school, where the teacher announced he was giving us our report cards sealed in an envelope. I did not care what incriminating evidence about my inability to pay attention in class was in the envelope. I walked out the front door, where I immediately saw Farooq leaning on his red-and-white bike. I walked by as if I did not see him. Of course, he followed me.

"Good evening, Laila. Need a ride today?"

I looked up, and for the first time, I saw his features. He was one shade darker than me, had a scar over his eyebrow, and sported slight hair growth on his lower face. He was handsome.

"Why do you stare and not answer me?" he asked. I smiled and walked away. He followed.

"Look, don't follow me!" I snapped. Something inside prevented me from being nice to that boy.

"What is wrong with you? Because you are pretty, you think you can treat me like this?" he yelled at me.

You think I am pretty? I thought. I started to regret treating him so rudely, and when he revved his bike to drive off, I said, "Farooq, I am sorry."

I accepted his offer and hopped on his bike, holding on tightly. We went to the shopping mall that day. As he weaved through traffic, I wondered what it would feel like to run away from home and never be in contact with my father again.

Farooq questioned me about my family, but I was very reluctant to share any information with someone I hardly knew. He was twenty years old and lived with his father while his mother commuted from Bahrain, where she worked as a nurse for the army. He kept looking down and refused to look at me when he discussed his family. I had seen that look before from Abeera and my aunt, both of whom were raped. I quickly told Farooq to take me home; as I worried my mother would notice my tardiness.

I felt comfortable with Farooq, so I kept sneaking out of the house to drink Pepsi with him. I spent that summer doing nothing but sleeping all day and watching television at night. Every other night, my little sister would join me. On those nights, we stayed up cooking whatever we could find to eat. Our favorite was rice and potatoes or rice and lentils.

Around July of that year, my father sent money, which was enough for us to look for a new home. We were happy we wouldn't have to cramp up in the one room in Nani's house anymore. We spent a week looking for an apartment in Karachi's Buffer Zone area and finally found a house with two bedrooms. It had rotted plumbing, and the electricity failed almost every other day, but other than that, it was clean with fresh paint.

We were on the first floor, and upstairs from us was a woman named Fatima and her two daughters, who were fourteen and sixteen. Her husband would show up occasionally from Dubai, where he worked. For the next two years, my mother constantly compared me to Fatima's daughters, telling me how pretty they were and how many men had come to ask for the older daughter's hand in marriage. Although they tried, I never allowed them to become my friends.

One day I grew sick of Mother's comments. "Why don't you kill Fatima and take her daughters for your own?" I snapped at her. She didn't answer.

Night after night, I fantasized about going to America. The nights my sister did not stay up with me, I became *Girl Six* for my father. After he finished masturbating, he always told me how hard he was working to get my visa. He had already been married to the woman for seven months. I wondered where she was while he was having phone sex. She must be as dumb as my mother, I thought.

I had graduated from high school. My father convinced Ammi it did not make sense for me to start university there in Karachi because it was only a matter of months before I would be an American resident.

September came, and while my siblings left for school, I sat in the house helping my mother take care of our new home, which now had some new things my mother bought with the American money my father sent. By November, he told me that he would be coming in December to bring me my Christmas present. After my mother found out he was coming, my siblings wrote lists of what they wanted him to bring for them. All I wanted was a visa to get out of Pakistan and leave all my bad memories behind. As the days grew closer to his arrival, my anxiety grew to where I did not sleep for two days.

No more pretending on the phone. He is on his way to do all the things he's talked about, I thought.

The day before he arrived, my mother spent extra time in the bathroom grooming for him. Ammi was excited that he was coming to be with her. It was like Allah was coming from the clouds above. The sad thing was that he was not coming for her; he was coming for me.

He came around 6:00 P.M. and was immediately stormed by my siblings running towards him with open arms. I stayed in the kitchen, pretending not to hear him come through the door. I walked out just in time to see him hugging and kissing my mother. I grew sick from the anxiety I felt and turned back to the kitchen and through the back door to get some air. I returned to the kitchen after taking a few deep breaths.

"Laila, your dad is here," Mother yelled.

He made his way to the kitchen with one of my little brothers tucked beneath his right hand. I walked towards him, and he grabbed me and hugged me. He went to the living room, where he opened a bag, taking out video games for my brothers and perfumes and slippers for Maya, Ammi, and me. My family was happy. I was not. I knew what the future held for me.

The first night he was there, he came into my room around 10:00 P.M. "Are you going to wait up for me? I miss you so bad," he said. He leaned over my bed and kissed me the same way he had kissed my mother when he entered the door earlier. I thought about how disappointed my mother would be if she knew why he'd returned.

I don't think he touched my mother that night because he ejaculated seconds after he started to have sex with me. I knew everything about becoming pregnant from nights and nights of *Sex in the City*, so I jumped out of the bed immediately, ran to the bathroom, and washed myself while sitting on the toilet.

For the next month, this happened at least twenty times. By the time he was ready to leave, I did not feel anything. My mind went to a different place when he did his evil to me. I don't know how I did not become pregnant. I don't think he cared if I were pregnant.

The second day after his arrival, the phone started ringing. "Can I speak to Abdul please?" came every other hour. At first my father told Maya and me to tell the woman he was staying at his brother's house, but when she started calling every hour during the day, and at 12:00 A.M., my mother became enraged and told her not to call so much.

"Who is the lady calling my house from America, Abdul? What is going on?" my mother finally asked when the woman called around 1:00 A.M.

He quickly hung up the phone and removed it from the wall. I was standing by the door along with Maya when I heard my mother cry out to Allah. Then she turned to my father, yelling and crying: "I waited for you in Mecca. I waited for you in Pakistan. And this is how you repay me, Abdulla? You are married? Allah will surely punish you like you never have been punished."

"I did it for our family" he said, in that whimpering voice he used to convince people he was not screwing them while they were bent over and not looking.

"You take a hammer and smash to pieces the little trust and hope I had in my hearts," she yelled. She cried for the next twenty-three days. Nothing quelled her pain. Ammi later told me how ashamed she felt.

My father left after thirty-one days, telling me at the door that he was getting the visa for me. "Only a matter of time," he said. We all sat at the door while his brother came and took him away. I thought it should have been a hearse picking up his dead carcass; but no, he got to go home to his second wife while we stayed there and suffered.

I was in trouble. I had no school, no friends, no life, and no idea what the future held for me. It became apparent to me that the only things that made me feel as if I were still among the living were the phone calls from my father and drinking Pepsi in the mall with Farooq. The phone calls were a reminder that I would not be stuck in this situation forever.

Chapter 15
America, Here I Come !

The phone call came around 10:00 P.M. Karachi time.

"I got the visa for you," he said. "Your uncle is going to pick you up about three weeks from now to bring you to the airport in Islamabad. Are you happy?"

I somehow knew after that phone call that there would be a good ending to my nightmare. For the next three weeks, I slept only four nights. Ask me to do something, and it was done; I cooked, cleaned, went to the market, took care of my brothers, and washed my sister's hair.

I did everything. It was the least I could do to thank Allah for delivering me from that twisted life. I wasn't going to miss being in Pakistan, and I was not even sure if I would miss anyone in my house. Maybe I wanted out of that life so badly that I could not miss anyone who was even remotely associated with it. I counted the days. I called Uncle Zafar to make sure of the date of my departure.

I became obsessed with counting the hours, and then the minutes, to my departure time. Anxiety and happiness devoured me. One night I used the money my father had given me, which I had saved for almost a year, to take a cab to my uncle's house just to see the ticket. I think the cab driver, my uncle, and his wife thought I was crazy for traveling alone so late at night.

"That is how women get kidnapped in Karachi!" my uncle said.

My mother had obviously called him, furious at me for leaving without telling her. I did not care one bit. What was my uncle going to punish me with? I had already suffered enough punishment at the hands of his family to last a lifetime.

The itinerary read: "2:00 P.M. departure, on United Emirates Airlines, from Jinnah Liaquat Airport, Karachi, to Dubai." From Dubai it was nonstop to London and then nonstop to Seattle. February 8 would become my release date from purgatory. My uncle stood there in the living room in awe while I jumped up and down as if I had won a million dollars. He looked so serious. I felt he was jealous that one of his children didn't have a visa for the United States instead. He and his wife really did not know why I was so happy. My mind went wild thinking of the details of my escape.

Maybe I can get off the plane in London and sneak out of the airport, I thought. Or maybe when I get off in Seattle, I can hide from my father and go my own way. The more I thought about my great escape, the more I realized I might not have the strength to pull it off. I would be on my own in an unfamiliar place.

Would I end up living on the street or having some pimp pick me up and return me to the life I knew? Those questions haunted me for the eight days before my departure. Two days before leaving, I became so stressed out that I snapped when my brother Saif found the book in which I had detailed how I felt about leaving Pakistan. My sister saved him that day, as I went insane and probably would have beaten him to death. He still has the scar over his eye from me punching his face so many times. He looked like my father, so once I started hitting him, I could not stop.

Poor Saif. He suffered that day, but when my mother came home, I suffered even more for hitting him. I had earned one of those beatings in which everything in the house became projectiles. Knives, cooking spoons, lamps, rolling pins, and the occasional food cans from the cupboard in the kitchen were all weapons. Ammi sometimes beat me and my siblings with various implements. This time she used the tongs for flipping *roti* over the fire. It was brutal. I had huge lumps all over my body for days.

"How dare you hit my son, huh!? *Badzaat larki!*" she yelled while administering blow after blow on my head and upper body. I believe the arthritis-like numbness and pain in both my hands today were caused by nerve damage from those beatings.

This is my final beating, I thought. She wants to kill me before I escape, or maybe disfigure or maim me to the point where I'll never have a husband and will be stuck with my family for the rest of my life.

After Ammi became physically tired, and the rage subsided, I was free to flee into the bathroom to assess the damage to my limbs. I had bruises on my hands, shoulders, and legs. There was so much adrenaline running through my veins that I couldn't possibly have felt pain.

I quickly made my way to the kitchen, which was beside the bathroom, and ran out the back door just in case she came back for more. It was like a scene out of a film on "Animal Planet," where people describe getting mauled by bears, escaping, and then trying to find a hiding place to prevent their rumps from being chewed off.

I closed the door and ran downstairs to my neighbor Fatima's door. Her younger daughter answered after the fourth knock. Fatima had just returned home from the government office where she worked as a clerk. She must have seen the terror in my eyes or heard the uproar above her head, because she quickly beckoned to me to come closer to her.

"Come here, poor girl," she said. As she walked closer, she must have noticed the bruises on my hands, but she pretended not to see them.

"What did you do, Laila? Tell me the truth," she said.

"I was beating up my brother because he read my book," I said, almost in tears. I was sad because, for the first time in my life, I had to tell someone why I abused my siblings. "I don't know why I hit him, because I love my brother very much. I don't know why I hit him," I repeated.

She looked at me and smiled, then looked down as if she needed time to make sense of the insanity she was hearing. "You don't know? Maybe it is because of what you have seen for most of your life."

When she said those words, I experienced a flashback in which all the abuse I had experienced came scrolling down like the credits from a movie.

After that, Fatima held me while I cried uncontrollably. I suddenly realized she was a total stranger and took two steps back, apologized for crying, and quickly made my way to the door.

"You can't keep running, Laila. You are going to have to face the truth," she shouted, as I scurried off toward my own apartment.

I turned and looked at her, thinking she must be a witch. I felt as though she knew everything about me, which scared me. Her house smelled like the nuts my uncle's wife always burned. We found out she fed her menses to her husband to make him stay with her, at least that's what my mother said. Her husband loved her dearly, although she was ugly as sin. I had never understood why he followed her around like a dog on a leash when he claimed to detest her face. Later on, he became a worthless bum and quit his job as a policeman, only to hang around his wife's buttocks. He got cancer and died five years after they were married. Fatima reminded me of a kinder version of my step-aunt, Zafar's wife.

She was a little too real for me, I thought. No problem. I wouldn't be dealing with her again ...

I sat on the back steps in pain for about an hour before I dared to enter the house. My sister came to the back door and whispered, "Ammi is asleep in Nani's room."

I went to our sleeping room. The adrenaline must have left my veins, because the pain from the beating started to riddle my body. My sister and brothers came over to the side of the area where I slept. My sister had painkillers in her hand, and my brother apologized for getting me into so much trouble.

"Don't worry. This is the last time she will ever beat me," I said.

They all huddled up beside me. All three begged me not to forget them, and my youngest brother asked me to behave so they could go to America, too. When my brothers fell asleep, my sister got down to business and inquired about my plans. Maya seemed most worried about my mental health.

"How are you going to live with that man?" she asked. "You have to find a way to leave him before you go mad."

As she spoke, I suddenly wondered why she had not slept in my bedroom in Mecca to protect me from our father. After all, she knew what had happened before. Those thoughts turned me off from sharing with her. In addition, the pills were finally taking effect. I explained that I was not sure what I would do, but I would find a way to escape the evil that awaited me. Maya kept talking, as usual. I pretended to fall asleep, which shut her up.

The next morning I awoke to my mother's voice. She was kneeling over the area on the floor where I slept, asking me to come eat breakfast.

"I don't want anything, Mom," I said, half asleep.

"Don't be mad at me and starve yourself," she said.

This was the only time I did not eat. Usually, I ate feverishly throughout the day to keep bad memories from surfacing, but I was only successful sometimes. I sat up, resting my back against the wall, and looked at her to see what kind of mood she was in. I could tell by her fake smile that she was not okay. I did not want to upset her any more. I feared she would do something to cause me to miss my flight. That was highly unlikely, but who knew what she was capable of when she was enraged? I quickly excused myself.

I normally sat in bed, deep in thought, for at least ten minutes before arising to eat breakfast. I usually woke up with the burden of my past eating my brain away, but this morning, the clock on the wall told me it was twenty-nine hours, forty-five minutes, and thirty-six ... thirty-five ... thirty-four seconds before my flight. This counting made me extremely happy. I folded my bedding neatly, brushed my teeth, and quickly went to the kitchen. I don't remember what was on the table, as my mind was engulfed with the thought of being on a plane to the land of LL Cool J and the girls from "Sex in the City."

I ripped pieces of *roti* to dip into some kind of meat, but I don't remember what it was. I quickly ate, stood up, and washed the dishes piled up in the sink from the night before. At my mother's request, I threw out any leftovers that were a day old. Ammi could have asked me to climb Mount Kilimanjaro that morning, and it would have been done. I had so much energy that I didn't need my usual two tea bags to wake me up for the day's chores. On other days, I boiled the tea until the water was pitch-black to squeeze out every ounce of caffeine.

I emptied the leftovers out the back door and sat at the kitchen table, hoping my mother would talk to me.

"Are you happy you're ridding yourself of me, Laila?" Ammi asked. As much as I wanted to tell her yes in order to make her feel the emotional pain I'd felt the night before, I could not.

"No, Ammi. I will miss you a lot," I said, tearing up. "You're my mother, and I love you." For the first time in years, tears flowed from her eyes for me.

"I love you, too, Laila, but sometimes life makes you do things you normally wouldn't do."

I knew she was referring to the mental abuse she had suffered at the hands of my father and his family. She would have been a better mother, to some extent, if it hadn't been for them. Maybe, I don't know. I had only heard stories from Nani and

Aunty Seema about how happy a person she was before she was shipped off to my father's house. "They killed her spirit," my aunty had said.

I forgave her for everything she had done because I knew what my father was capable of. He had ruined my chance for a good childhood in every way possible. I hugged my mother tightly and told her I would be back to get her as soon as I could.

I knew my father had no plans to have her ever leave Pakistan. Why would he need a broken soul following him around in the United States? He had sucked the life out of my beautiful mother, leaving only her carcass to exist in torment. He had hardly ever taken her anywhere and almost never asked her if she was okay. Instead, he spent most of his time worrying about every detail of my life.

The night before I left Pakistan, nothing could stop my brain from counting. "Fourteen hours, five minutes, and twenty-one seconds ..." When I could not stop watching the clock, I turned on American television. No sleep that night. As I watched TV, I thought of the opportunity awaiting me to become free. Around 5:30 A.M., my father called to check that I was ready to leave.

"Are you ready to come? I am waiting for you," he said in that sleazy voice he used when talking about sex. I quickly told him yes.

My mother had heard the phone ring and made her way to the living room, where I had been sitting all night long. Covering the receiver so he wouldn't hear me, I handed it to her. "Here Ammi, the phone," I whispered. He was still talking when she took it. I don't know why I did this. I guess I wanted her to know what a disgusting man he was, so she would never miss him.

"Now we can do whatever we want, whenever we want," he said.

"Why do you sound like this, Abdulla?" she asked.

My plan hadn't worked! He explained that he was only talking about my education and that I could do whatever I wanted with an American degree.

She believed him and continued to talk. "Take care of my daughter. Don't let anything happen to her," she said.

Eight hours, ten minutes, and forty-four seconds left ...

I kept counting until I fell asleep from exhaustion. Later Uncle Zafar woke me by yelling that my flight was soon. He was there to take me to the airport. I jumped up so fast that I hurt my back. Everyone in our house knew I was leaving go to America, so it was time for the ritual of watching every item I packed in my suitcase.

I had six outfits, but every piece I put in the bag drew attention. Every article packed produced comments about where I would wear it. My mother's brother, my Uncle Asif, whom I really loved, commented on how cheap my bag looked. "You can't go to America like that. Seema, give her one of the bags you got from your sister."

Seema was in the kitchen with my mother, preparing snacks for my forty-four-hour trip. She yelled back at him in what had become her trademark sarcastic tone. "She is going to America's Seattle, so she can buy several bags when she gets there."

My uncle answered, "You give her the money. I know you have hidden the U.S. dollars your sister sent you from Michigan."

Just before I left the house, Uncle Asif gave me one hundred U.S. dollars and said, "Keep this for a rainy day."

I finished packing the six outfits. My mother handed me an eight-and-a-half-by-eleven-inch sealed manila envelope containing information from the United States Embassy. "Guard this envelope like it is your unborn child," she said. "Don't dare to open it. When you get to the U.S., give it to the immigration officer."

My bag had no zipper, so you could see the top of the envelope sticking out of the bag. Maya started to cry, looking at me as if she wanted to come with me. Uncle Zafar, realizing that she was sad, offered to take her with us to the airport.

"Okay," she said, jumping up and down. "I'll go get my shoes," she added in her typical, fast-paced voice. She ran to the car, hurrying for fear my uncle might have a change of heart. There was not a dry eye in our house that afternoon. My mother held me, crying; my aunt comforted my little brothers; and even Uncle Asif wept.

Suddenly, the desire to leave almost disappeared, and all I could think about were the good times I'd spent with my family before the sorcerer started molesting me. I walked to the car and never looked back. I was done with Karachi, Pakistan, and soon I would be done with my father's filthy lifestyle. My uncle's old, yellow cab drove down the dirt road that led to my school, where I left Farooq and Nida behind, and Maya stared up at me with pride, smiling ear to ear.

"You're going on the big plane by yourself, eh? Just remember who is in charge of your life now. It is not Abdul anymore. It is you!" she whispered.

I stared at her proudly, thinking, "Look at this little girl telling me how to live my life!"

My uncle gave me about ten different instructions for transferring from one plane to the next, none of which I remembered, but I recalled every word Maya said. I got out of the yellow cab, kissed and hugged her good-bye, and thanked my uncle for picking up my visa and taking me to the airport.

I boarded the plane in Karachi after going through metal detectors, customs officers, and ticket agents. I felt proud when I told the customs officer my final destination was Seattle.

I sat in the seat assigned to me and immediately had a flashback to the last time I had traveled, the trip from Mecca. On that flight, my mother had looked scared, not knowing what was ahead of us, while my brothers and Maya talked constantly about seeing their cousins in Pakistan. I made Ammi laugh by saying, "At least those *Hajji* people didn't skin us alive." I continued to cheer her up by talking about our near-death experience. "They were going to come through the little hole where the air conditioner was, Ammi! They were out for our asses!"

I laughed to myself, thinking of her smile. Her face was round and chubby, and when she smiled, her cheeks lit up like those of the Pillsbury Dough Boy I had seen in a commercial. The thought of having only forty-four hours until I arrived in America brought me peace and happiness I had never felt before.

While I waited twelve hours in London Heathrow airport for the next flight, I met a lady named Sonya, who was traveling from Dubai to New York. She was

Muslim, but she looked like someone right out of a Hollywood movie: Louis Vuitton hand luggage, Chanel shades resting on the top of her head, and a black leather outfit from head to toe. I don't know why she chose to speak to me, but Sonya gave me some good advice.

"Don't forget you're not in Pakistan anymore," she said. "You live life to the fullest, and if you ever need a hand with anything, call me, and I will help you." Minutes later, she offered me her phone number and told me how she had acquired everything on her own, including a loft in New York.

"A pretty girl like you can make three thousand dollars U.S. a night," she said.

Somehow I knew what that entailed. I thought about it for a second before my flight was announced. "British Airways, nonstop to Seattle, leaving from gate 24b." I quickly rose from my seat, not wanting Sonya to give me her phone number. I was afraid I would use it once I arrived in Seattle.

I endured the strip search and a thorough search of my belongings to get on the plane. I was not offended, because a woman did the search. I now learned first-hand what "homeland security" was all about. All those American television shows and movies must have made me forget I was Muslim. The nice customs officer stuck her hands up my burqa, touching my crotch, my back, and my breasts. I did not feel violated.

There was a slight crack in the Jet-way that led to entrance of the plane when I boarded the Seattle flight. Never before had I felt such a chill. The pilot said it was twelve degrees Fahrenheit outside. I sat in seat 16A, a window seat.

The plane took off, and about five minutes later, I closed my eyes and went to sleep. I woke up over American soil when the pilot announced we were one hour away from the airport in Seattle. I spent half an hour at immigrations. I handed the immigrations officer the big, brown envelope and became a permanent resident alien of the United States.

When I was free to go from immigrations, I became panic-stricken. I thought about how long my 120 U.S. dollars would last if I decided to run away. I walked out of the terminal, and before I could even think about diverting to some place my father would not find me, I saw him walking towards me. His new wife waited behind him with balloons and flowers in her hands.

The woman was no taller than my five-foot mother and weighed around 270 pounds, with buttocks the size of Texas. She introduced herself as my new mother. I had mixed feelings about that. She was the one who had made it easy for me to get a visa out of Karachi, but she was also responsible for breaking my mother's heart. Why had she called so often? My mother was so naïve that she would never have known what was going on. The woman hugged me, and it started right there in the airport — another person I was going to have to pretend to love.

"This is your stepmother, Deborah," my father said. She smiled at me as though I were a delicious piece of pastry. Deborah had short hair and was in her forties. She looked like Rosie O'Donnell, the talk show host I had seen on American television.

"Come, let's get your bags. You must be tired after the long trip," she said. My father looked at me sternly, silently asking why I wasn't answering the lady. I was as serious as a judge handing out a life sentence. My green suitcases sat on the side of baggage claim, along with another bag I knew belonged to a Nigerian lady on the plane. She was still being grilled by custom officers about her visa. My father picked up my bags and carried them to the car, while Deborah went on and on about how happy she was to have a new daughter.

It was raining in Seattle, which was not surprising, according to the research I had done to find a place to run away to after getting off the plane. Deborah made it clear that the Chrysler we piled into was *her* car when she told me not to mess up the car mats with mud. After an hour passed, I thought Seattle must be really big because it seemed like we drove forever.

Finally, I knew we were not in Seattle anymore when went over "the pass," a highway through mountains full of snow and ice. After Deborah complained she was hungry, we stopped in a town called Auburn to get food from my father's friend.

We traveled through the town for about ten minutes and pulled up in front of a closed Indian restaurant. My father walked through its side door, and a few minutes later, he emerged with another, well-shaved Pakistani man.

"I am Sam. What's your name, pretty lady?" he asked me. I tried to smile but couldn't because fear of the unknown was too overwhelming.

I did not trust my father, and I was unsure what his plans were for me. I would not have been surprised had he sold me into slavery for money. This sorcerer is capable of anything, I thought.

"Come, let's get something to eat." Sam showed us into the restaurant and opened its shutters. It was 10:30 P.M. My father quickly walked behind the counter and cooked up some buttered chicken with rice. I had not eaten much on the trip—just a few snacks from the London airport—so I quickly prepared a plate for myself. I devoured the food quickly with my fingers while Deborah did the same using a fork, looking up at me every other minute.

"I don't know why you people have to use your hands to eat," she said. "I will teach you how to use a knife and fork."

I was appalled.

"Everyone in my country eats this way," I answered, speaking to her for the first time.

"Well, that's not how we do it in America, and you're in the U.S. now, so you have to learn our way of doing things."

This was the first of about a thousand times I would have to endure "you-people-now-you're-in-the-U.S." from her during the next year.

My father brought me a pair of his corduroy pants and a jacket from the trunk of the car because by then I was visibly trembling from the cold. It was freezing. The clothes I had worn on the plane were suitable only for Karachi. I put his clothes on in the restaurant bathroom and emerged quickly, fearing my father or his friend would head in any minute.

After we ate, we went back in the car, thanked Sam for the food, and resumed the trek to what was to become my new prison. After driving past a sign that read "Ellensburg," Deborah turned her head in my direction in the back seat. "Only forty minutes left, Laila," she said. We pulled into a town called Selah around 12:20 AM.

The house was the smallest one on the block, which was on Ninth Avenue. I got out of the car while Deborah stood over me, smiling. "You're home," she said. My father took my bags from the trunk. We quickly made it to the door, running out of the cold and into the house. It was cold, but not as frigid as Auburn had been. I walked through the door into a small kitchen, and after exactly three steps, I was in the living room.

"Do Mama Smurf and Papa Smurf live here?" I wondered. I immediately noticed I had entered a living shrine to Barbie. Before I could digest the amount of Barbie memorabilia that riddled the living room, Deborah's dog Brandy rushed through the bedroom door. It scared the living hell out of me. I did not expect to see a dog in a house. I must have jumped five feet in one leap, holding my broken handbag to shield me from the attack.

"She is harmless. She doesn't bite," Deborah assured me. I later went into her room where there were four cats lying on the bed. A few days later, I started wheezing uncontrollably because of those animals.

Deborah's bedroom also contained more dolls and Teddy bears than a toy store. My father must feel so out of place here, I thought. Good! Punish him, Allah.

"These are worth a lot of money," Deborah said, picking up one of the vintage Barbie dolls still in its original box.

I did not want to see or hear about any toys at that moment. I was busy wondering how and when I would finally get a chance to escape the insanity. "Okay. I'm going to bed now," I said, turning away from her. "I am tired."

"I already put some comforters for you on your bed," she said. It was a fold-up bed in the living room across from a computer desk, computer, and television.

Chapter 16
Psychological Warfare

Deborah's home would become my new hell. She played ping-pong and other computer games or watched television with her friends while I tried to sleep. Sitting on the couch, I took off the extra clothes I had worn for almost two days, while my father went outside to smoke. I realized that this house was under the control of one "man:" Deborah. My father had smoked in our house in Pakistan since I was a child, but he didn't dare to do so in this house. He could not even leave the toilet seat up there.

I used Deborah's strictness to my advantage, and when he came that night for what he wanted from me, I yelled, "That woman is not going to let you do that in her house," as he hovered over my body like a wolf smelling meat. I meant business. I called her name as loudly as I could, while he tried to put his hands over my mouth.

"What are you trying to do?" he whispered. "You can't do that here. I bring you to America, and this is what you do to me? You will pay for this." As he walked away, I shouted, "Try doing what you did in Pakistan, and I will call the cops. I watch American TV. I know how it is here." Once I'd set foot on American soil, I felt a new confidence. I swore my life was going to change.

Not long after, my mother called to make sure I had arrived safely. Deborah answered and brought me the phone. "Yes, Ammi, I am here," I said.

"Okay, okay, I'll let you sleep. I just wanted to see if you got there safely," she said.

I handed the phone back to Deborah, who was visibly upset that my mother had called. I did not sleep much because I was filled with pride that I had stood up to my father. I was elated for days to come. I started to watch television after he left and went into the kitchen to see what the fridge had to offer. I was amazed by the plethora of unhealthy food choices. I ate everything I saw, became colicky, and had to use Nida's trick to regurgitate food. At first, I tried the many fruits I hadn't seen since leaving Saudi Arabia, including two different types of apples and peaches. Then I ate three types of ice cream along with left-over *biryani*. I gained twenty-five pounds within two months after arriving in Selah, Washington.

As I expected, anything my father cooked up was one big pot of filth for me. I did nothing but clean Deborah's house, as she made it clear I was going to be her personal maid from a third-world country. Deborah's expectations quickly became my new nightmare. She also bossed my father around.

"Can you make me some tea, walk Brandy, and make sure dinner is ready when I get home? That's the least you can do after all I am doing for your family," she told him, always expecting whatever she asked to be done promptly.

Deborah quickly made it clear I was going to be the daughter she never had. "We're going to get you into the college down the road. I'm going to get you some really nice clothes to wear — nothing too revealing, of course," she said.

"Okay, sounds good," I said. My mind went wild thinking what was next for me. New clothes, new life … I'd quickly find a handsome man to marry and get out of Deborah's house. The "nice clothes" she talked about never came, however, and the stuff she bought me was frumpy and ugly.

It was February, so I had to wait almost a month before the spring quarter started at the college. During that time, I fought with my father almost every night, and every night it became worse. I was like a boxer in the ring, and he was the opponent trying to wear me down round after round. He was like a pack of hyenas trying to figure out the best vantage point from which to attack.

At first he threatened, "I'll send you back home to your mother." When that did not work, he said, "I'm going to rip up your passport and have Deborah put you on the street."

That was at night. During the day when Deborah was at work, he took the friendly approach and came bearing gifts like the Three Wise Men, as if I were Jesus Christ.

"I know you must miss home, so I brought you some food from the restaurant" or "some Indian music." Or he offered, "You must be bored; let me take you shopping at the mall." Food was his favorite bribe.

After about three weeks of all that nonsense, none of which worked, he decided to take a different approach. It was Deborah's day off on a rainy Thursday when he came in looking like the dogs you see in those animal shelter commercials begging to be saved from euthanasia. "I passed out at work today. My diabetes flared up," he said, as he walked through the door.

Ammi had told me he suffered from diabetes, and I had seen him taking insulin shots, but I didn't care. At least, I thought I didn't care, until I realized that he was still the primary breadwinner in my family.

After he told his sob story about how the ambulance came but he refused to go to the hospital, Deborah went on a tirade about how he needed to take better care of himself.

I went outside to catch some air after feeling suffocated by the heap of garbage being said.

Everything was brown, and all the trees on the mountains surrounding Selah were bare. There were also white patches of snow covering the brown earth. I had thought I would find lush, green trees everywhere, as I had seen in the movies. This difference served as a reminder that, so far, things were not what I expected. At the same time, I was comfortable with the progress I had made. I tried not to think about my father or his ailments, but it was futile.

I went back in the house and soon noticed that he and Deborah had retired to the bedroom.

"Laila, Laila, can you come in here, please?" she called. "I'm going to teach you how to check your father's sugar levels and give him shots."

"What? I can't do that!" I objected.

As I walked into her memorabilia-filled bedroom, I saw his face. It was a look I had never seen before. His eyes were half-closed, looking at me as if we had some hidden code that Deborah couldn't understand.

"Come on, take the needle," she insisted. I took it and gave him an insulin shot in his stomach. For five seconds, I wished the syringe were filled with arsenic or tainted blood from an Ebola-virus-filled jungle animal. Part of me, though, felt sorry for him. In some weird way, I was still connected to this man. I tried to understand this then; I've tried to understand it now; and I still don't get it.

The next morning, I was awakened by a huge thump. I had a full view of the bathroom from my pull-out bed in Deborah's living room. My father was sprawled out on the floor like a man I had seen in the Pakistani market gunned down by a merchant from whom he'd tried to steal. My father was on his face. I jumped up and ran to the bathroom.

"Deborah, come, come!" I yelled.

I certainly did not know what to do. As I knelt over him, I shook him to wake him up.

Allah, please, don't let him die! At least keep him alive until I can work and take care of Ammi, I thought. I shook him so hard he awoke and immediately asked me to help him sit up against the door.

"Deborah!" I yelled.

"She's at work. Don't worry. I'll be okay," he said. "Help me to the bedroom." He slowly stood up and rested his hand on my shoulder. It was not even a minute after he hit the mattress before he started asking me to lie in the bed beside him.

"Laila, I am dying. Bring me some water. Come lie beside me. Keep me company when you come back."

I walked to the kitchen, thinking this man could very well die. I felt bad for him. I drank some water and returned to the bedroom. I sat on the side of the bed where he beckoned me with his head to lie down. It wasn't long before he was doing the same things that usually happened when we were in bed together, and I no longer felt the hatred. You should know better than to let your guard down, said the voice inside me.

A week later, I started school at the local community college in Yakima. My plans changed from the original idea of leaving Deborah's house with the man of my dreams to just appeasing everyone who lived in her home. Several guys must have seen me as fresh meat at the community college, but I ignored everyone except the girls in my ESL (English as Second Language) class reading groups. All of them were Mexican and new in America like me. We had something in common: none of us could communicate with the rest of our classmates.

Forty percent of Yakima's population was Mexican. Deborah complained about all the "wetbacks who are stealing the good resources." Their ancestors had migrated to the United States as farm workers, and now they seemed to own everything from restaurants to huge houses on Selah mountainsides.

After the second quarter of beginners' courses for immigrants in English and math, school became a bore; there was nothing there for me. The math I already knew was far more advanced, and I couldn't understand my English teachers because they spoke too fast. I had never thought I could become more depressed than I had been in Pakistan.

I was two hundred miles from the nearest big city. Nothing had changed about my torturous life. On top of that, I was living with a crazy woman, who, I swore, was actively trying to have me for herself. When my father went to work at his fledgling restaurant, Deborah talked my ears off about "not needing a man." By summer, Deborah trusted me enough to show me her more-than-fifty sex toys. She had everything, including vibrators, fake male parts, golden-looking eggs that vibrated, and a big black penis she called "Mandingo." Mandingo, she said, gave her "G orgasms."

"You put this right here," she said, exposing herself and demonstrating how to use it. Her exposing herself to me was no big deal, since I had seen women making out together on the porn shows my father forced me to watch as a child.

"Here, take them and use them whenever you want," Deborah offered.

I was now nineteen and had never made love to a man. For the next two years, Deborah's sex toys were an escape to my own reality. I never used her astronomical dildos, but I tried every one of her vibrators. My first orgasm felt as though all the blood from my body had rushed to my crotch. I became an addict who used those toys five to six times a day. I lived in the bathroom, where I sat on the floor and braced my feet on the side of the tub.

Deborah and I had two things in common at the time—we both disliked like men, and we did not need them.

"I just wanted to help your father bring your family here, but I don't need him for anything. He can't do much anyway because of his diabetes," she stated one evening as she whipped out a new rabbit vibrator she bought from an online store. As for me, after having multiple orgasms via vibrators and still having to give my father oral sex, I became a true man-hater like Deborah.

She told me about the first person she had fallen in love with. It was her best friend from high school who was a woman whose advances she had turned down several times. Her friend then ended up falling in love and living with another woman.

"I should've gone with Patty," she would say realizing she had made a mistake marrying a man. It reminded me of my little run-in with Nida and made me question my own sexuality.

Sometimes, while talking about sex and masturbating, Deborah would pour me some of her private collection of vodka and Cognac. Within months, I was stealing it to make myself numb after dealing with my father. Doing things with him had become a chore like washing the dishes, but in my heart, I knew I was losing a piece of myself every time I was with him.

At night, I watched *"Sex in the City"* and hip-hop videos as an escape from my life. After Deborah found me watching those videos, I shared with her that I liked black men.

"I like them, too," she said, "but I don't trust black people. I see them looking at my big ass in the malls. They love big asses. This one guy who worked as a mechanic where I got my oil changed always hit on me. I would only think about him while I masturbated. Girls who are not black who want to be with black guys just want them because they have huge dicks and stamina of steel."

After that, I realized she was not only racist but an idiot. I knew she was against black culture when I tried to watch the movie *Diary of a Mad Black Woman*. I had to watch it in six different pieces because, according to her, "They are stupid shows made by stupid people." I turned it off every time she came into the living room but quickly turned it on after she left. When I tried to tell her that my father and I were not white, she said, "You are not black. You are brown and Asian." The amount of garbage she sprayed out of her mouth could have filled up the city's landfill across town.

"What in Allah's name is going to get me out of this cycle of madness?" I often thought to myself.

After six months of listening to her with no escape in sight, I began killing time in the school's different labs — writing labs, math labs, computer labs — I would have been in the meth labs the police constantly busted up almost daily if I'd known where to find one. I started smoking — only cigarettes, though, except for marijuana just one time. I went to a party where everyone was smoking pot, including a new Indian friend who disappeared on me, leaving me at the mercy of those crazy druggies.

I started buying liquor when I knew I would be home alone. When I couldn't be by myself at home, I went down by the Yakima River, which ran through our town, and drank and smoked Marlboro Lights until my sorrows went away. I stayed out more and more, and the calls on my cell phone from Deborah came more often.

"Laila, where are you? Buy me Reese's candy, cookie dough ice cream, or Hershey's kisses," or her main treat, sunflower seeds. When she needed something from the "gofer," she called me.

Deborah soon made it clear I needed to find a job to "make ends meet," because now "we have an extra mouth to feed." Within weeks, I found a job at the local ice cream parlor. Unfortunately, it only lasted one day because the Indian owner tried to grab my buttocks. Weeks later, I found a job as a front desk agent in a local hotel and became the "pretty girl who worked like a slave," according my co-worker.

At home, I cooked dinner, and after eating, Deborah and her friends just got up, leaving the dishes at the table. If I didn't clean them, she screamed the next day that she had to come home from work to a dirty house. All the housework now became my job, and as for my scum of a father, his restaurant failed due to lack of customers. He now sat at home waiting for me to arrive and serve him. Homework was not important because, according to Deborah, I was only attending community college.

I now been living in the United States several years, and every day, it became harder for me to survive. I started to miss Pakistan and being with my mother.

"I thought you said she was going to do everything," I heard Deborah whine to my father one day after she returned home from work.

It was then that I realized my mother had treated me better than I had thought. I had so much resentment for her that when I grew older, I forgot the good times when she had taken care of me. The fighting escalated in Deborah's house after I became openly resentful at catering to everyone on a daily basis. I started to do whatever I could to let them know I was not happy with my life. According to them, I was just being an "ungrateful little bitch." Meanwhile, my father started to use my sister's visa as collateral to bribe me to do whatever he wanted.

Life in Selah, Washington, was progressively more horrendous. Deborah became intoxicated one night and talked about how much pain she had suffered in her life and how beautiful I was. She begged me to lie down on her bed, stripped, and asked to see my body naked. I felt sorry for her as she cried about how lonely she had been most of her life. I did what I knew best. I took my clothes off, lay in the bed, and let her touch me all over until her mouth ended up in my crotch. She stuffed her face down there and told me, "I've wanted to do this ever since you walked into my life." I felt nothing and lay there motionless until she was done, which seemed like forever. She really loved doing it, and afterwards, she grabbed her vibrator and had a "monster orgasm," according to her. She did what she wanted, just as my father had done for years.

Is everyone in my life going to use my body for their pleasure? I asked myself. When am I ever going to stop this madness? When am I going to have someone I can have pleasure being intimate with?

I did not go home after school the next day. It was late November, and leaves were everywhere. I sat in the park by the river, wishing I had a canoe to paddle my way out of Shit Creek, Washington. I sat there in the cold until all the feeling left my toes, lips, and fingers. I drank the half-bottle of Smirnoff I had stolen from Deborah's secret stash. When I finally couldn't stand the cold anymore, I started to walk aimlessly through the park in the dark. I became frightened when the bushes rustled a few feet from me. I took off running toward the street lights. Then I walked to the main road, trudged along for a mile, and turned on the block where Deborah's house stood. Trouble met me at the door.

"You want to be a whore and screw every man in Yakima, huh?!" Deborah screamed. "Well, here is your stuff. But if you're going to go, I'm sending your dad with you so you won't be tramping around town alone."

She threw my belongings on the front lawn. She followed with my father's passport and green card, along with his clothes. Then she grabbed him by his shirt and pushed him out the front door.

I felt hopeless at that point. "What else, Allah, what else can you do to test me?" I yelled. "What kind of evil person am I for you to do this to me?"

The neighbors looked on in disgust from their front yards. My father quickly gathered our stuff and threw it in his green Dodge. Deborah later told me she sent my father's friends to look for us on First Street because she knew we had no money to leave town. These friends took us to their house, where Deborah called as much as she had when my father visited Pakistan.

After two days in the friends' house, Deborah invited us back to her house. When I arrived home, she was in bed hugging and kissing my father. As soon she saw me, she came running towards me.

"I'm sorry, Laila. You know I love you. You are my daughter. Now, please forgive me for losing my temper."

I knew this lady was broken and irreparable, so I gave in to her pleas, hugging her back. For the next two days, things were okay. Then I did not answer my cell phone when Deborah called me. Instead, I went to the house and jumped into bed, pretending to be asleep when she walked in the door. She was talking on her cell phone—on the speaker phone—with my father.

"She didn't answer the phone. She obviously thinks she can do whatever she wants to do," she derided.

My father's voice asked Deborah, "Do you think she is still a virgin? Do you think she's having sex?" Why would he ask her that question? What was he trying to do?

"Yeah! When virgins have sex, they go crazy for it," Deborah replied.

"When I get home, I'll deal with her," he said.

My pillow was soaked with tears. His question was the last straw for me. I decided to leave the house permanently.

For two days, I did nothing. No school, no gofer duties, nothing. I called my mother the second day, crying, as I usually did after my father yelled at me for what Deborah called my "ungratefulness for bringing me here from a third-world country."

As my mother listened on the phone, my father called me unspeakable names, but one stuck out: whore. After all that man had done to me, he called me a whore! He and Deborah sat there yelling, while my mother quietly listened to everything. It took a week for me to get a ticket back to Pakistan. My mother called a family friend in Seattle who put the ticket on his credit card.

The day before I left, my father came home from work and asked me to get him a glass of juice. After I brought it, he asked, "Please help me take my pants off. My knees hurt." He sat on the couch, and I bent to remove the pants.

"Anything else you want?" I asked.

The first kick landed me on the ground. Then he stood up and commenced a barrage of kicks into my gut. I tried to fold up into a fetal position to protect my face and vital organs, which made him rotate and kick me in the back.

"If you want to talk to me like you're my maid, then I'll treat you like a maid!" he screamed.

I crouched, motionless, unable to cry. The insult of him beating me like a slave made me felt less than dirt. As he left for the bedroom, I thought about going out to the main road and walking into a truck, but I couldn't make it to the door. I was numb. Something happened to my brain like before, but this was more extreme. I couldn't cope anymore. My brain went haywire, and I could not reset it.

I don't remember getting into the car or driving to the airport. I do remember my father and Deborah yelling at me at the airport and handing me my bags. I woke up after four hours of an eight-hour layover. My brain roused as soon as I realized I had blood running down my legs. I had a flashback of the night I ran to my grandmother's room. I had no money, so

I ended up asking an Indian lady for a pad in the London airport. She looked at me as if I were crazy, grabbed her baggage, and walked off as though I had asked for her firstborn child. A blonde girl next to her must have heard me, because she handed me a tampon. I had not eaten for two days and was nauseated from the bleeding and hunger. It took twenty more hours to get to Karachi.

My mother met me at the airport, crying. She said they were tears of joy, but I knew better. I had returned bearing no gifts for my family, only a broken brain. My sister later told me I talked to myself in the kitchen while I cleaned and cooked obsessively. I had lost control of my senses. On my good days, I stared out the window, waiting for my sister to come home from school and doing whatever it took to make her happy. Maya told me that I talked myself to sleep for the next five months. Then a woman came to our house asking my mother to arrange a meeting with a local boy who had four sisters for whom he needed to pay the dowry. He wanted to marry me because I had an American visa. When I heard this, it was as if a bell went off in my head, ringing, "More users! More users!"

I had a month left on the six months I was allowed to be out of the country on my visa. My father telephoned, and Maya answered. She would not even talk to him. She flung the phone at me after hearing his voice.

"Laila, if you don't come back to the U.S., you won't ever be able to return," he said. He told me he'd left Deborah's house and was now in Chicago working as a taxi driver with Nazir. Things would be different. "I promise," he insisted. I don't know why, but I believed him. Soon I was on a plane back to the U.S. with my original plan intact.

Chicago is a big city, like New York. Things should be better for me this time around, I thought.

Chapter 17
The Hanging In Chicago

My father picked me up from the airport in the taxi he rented to make money. He looked weak, emaciated, and troubled. His eyes had sunk into their sockets as if he were a corpse. He obviously was not taking care of himself or his diabetes. After a week of caring for him without him making any advances, I started to believe things had changed. I loved Chicago. Enough people were around to keep me from thinking so much. I planned to work and get my own apartment in the city.

About a week after I arrived, I acquired a job at the corner store my father's friend owned. The store was located in the South Side of Chicago. Clusters of dilapidated buildings called "the projects" by locals stood everywhere. The apartments all had grills on the windows and hundreds of people hanging out in front of them. I felt right at home. Random gunfire didn't scare me; this was normal everyday life back home. It was just like Karachi.

Work at the store was difficult because I was never allowed to sit. I worked harder than I had ever worked in my life, but it felt good to be around so many people of color. They walked in the store mainly to buy Lotto tickets. Most of them had such colorful personalities that I thought about their behavior long after they were gone.

My father's friend's studio apartment, where we were staying, was on a quiet street in front of a cemetery. It had three floors and twenty-six units. One night when I arrived home from work after a thirteen-hour day, the sorcerer was on the phone with my mother in Karachi. He handed the receiver to me.

"Ammi, I am so tired. My feet hurt so much from standing all day," I said.

While I talked to her on the phone, my father bent down and slowly removed my shoes and socks. I wondered what in the hell he was up to. He went into bathroom, brought back lotion, bent down, and started to apply it to my feet. Ammi was telling me she was not doing well physically, but she didn't want me to worry. My father kept rubbing my feet. They hurt so bad, it felt good when his warm hands massaged them. I told Ammi good-bye and stretched out in the recliner.

The last time my father had done something like that was in Pakistan when I hurt myself playing soccer in the yard at age six. He put some kind of magic oil on my feet and rubbed the pain away. Now he continued to massage my feet until I almost fell asleep. I became somewhat alert when I felt the long, black skirt I wore moving up towards my knees along with his hands.

In between sleep and wakefulness, I enjoyed his massage, so I obliviously continued to lie there until I felt something wet on my leg. While kissing my thigh, he had already made his way to my underwear. Using my hands on the side of the chair for leverage, I thrust my legs forward and sent him tipping over onto his buttocks.

"I can't trust you for a minute, you poor excuse for a father, you nasty pervert!" I screamed. "Don't you ever touch me again, or I will kill you! Do you hear me? I'll kill you and then kill myself!" I went on for about ten minutes.

"You filthy beast," I continued. "You want your own daughter to be your sex slave? Ha! You want to screw me until you go to the grave? How long? How long! Fifteen years you've taken my body and mind. You've turned my life into a nightmare in which I try killing myself, cutting myself, betraying my mother! How long? No more! No more, man!"

A memory of my mother's Pillsbury Dough Boy-shaped face crying outside the airport in Pakistan made me angrier. I continued my venting for another five minutes, yelling out expletives in intervals, as if I had Tourette's syndrome.

"Filthy beast! Soap scum! Sex-hungry psycho! Nasty son of a bitch! Sick fuck!" Those were just a few of the names I can recall.

I made up my mind that his traps would not catch me this time around. He must have seen the fire in my eyes. He turned away and cried, telling me how much he needed me, how sick he was, and how much he loved me.

"Yes, you are a sick fuck!" I said.

I went to lie down on the bed in the living room, exhausted from my grandstanding. It had taken every ounce of strength I had. I must have fallen asleep immediately, leaving him sitting where he had landed on the floor. Until this day, I'm not sure what woke me up—whether it was natural or whether he did something to rouse me. I found him in the kitchen with a belt around his neck tied to the pipe in the ceiling that led to the heat in the upstairs apartment. He wore only his underwear, and his tongue was hanging out. His feet leaned on the kitchen counter, and he held onto the belt with both hands. His head hung down like that of Jesus crucified on the cross. It was the worst thing I had ever seen in my life.

I screamed, "No! No! No, Allah! You can't do this to me!"

I grabbed a knife from the set in a cupboard drawer, jumped on the counter, and cut the belt after five swipes. He fell on the ground. I leapt off the countertop and grabbed his face to see if he was breathing. After about three seconds, he gasped for air and opened his eyes. I started to bawl hysterically. He told me he had done it because he loved me so much and I wouldn't love him back.

That was the last thing I remember before my brain blacked out again. I woke up the next morning wearing the skirt I had worn to work the day before, but no underwear, and the blouse I had worn, but no brassiere. I knew what had happened, but I didn't specifically remember a thing. I did not go to work. I couldn't. My lips were too swollen, and I had marks all over my body, especially my neck, as if I'd been attacked by an animal. I never said no to him after that day. I always let him do whatever he wanted.

After months of working to pay the bills and sending money home for my family, I had nothing but the clothes I had brought from Pakistan and my work uniform. I never went out. I didn't take care of myself and never looked in the mirror. I started drinking more heavily and became a mindless slave for my father and my family.

Good-looking guys tried to talk to me at the store, but I was too far gone. "I'm just trying to spit game to you, Shorty — let me take you home to my mama, take you out of this place. You will never work another day in your life, baby."

These were some of their pick-p lines used which made me laugh most of the times. They would come back to the store to buy the most insignificant things just to talk to me. Those days were the highlight of my time in Chicago. Too traumatized by what my father had done, I did not respond to their advancces. I could not return the attention they gave me, although I wanted to.

After working for months, giving sixty percent of his earnings to the owner of the cab, the sorcerer decided he'd had enough. We still had our cell phones, since Deborah had never cut them off. She called six or seven times a day, begging us to come back. Although I knew she was a bad person, I felt sorry for her, and I usually answered when she called.

My father used the cell phone to call in our surrender back to Selah. By then, I was not even a person anymore. I was a drone who only wanted to make sure my mother and siblings did not end up on the street.

Deborah had taken back the Chrysler she had lent me, so we returned to Selah on the Greyhound bus after traveling for two days through Wisconsin, Minnesota, the Dakotas, Montana, and Idaho. I sat there, mindless, wondering what was to become of my senseless life.

Deborah now had a brand-new home built with insurance money she received when her small cottage burned down. When I arrived in Selah, I was so tired that Deborah's living room felt like a five-star hotel. I ate some leftover pasta and quickly went into the second bedroom and threw myself on the bed. I said nothing to her because I was too ashamed. I felt like a dog returning to eat his own vomit.

I woke up the next morning in search mode, thinking of what I could do to get away from this woman and this man. I took on two jobs and registered for the upcoming quarter at school, which started in four weeks. Sometimes I worked nineteen hours a day. I used cigarettes to block sleep from my eyes when I felt tired. When I finished working and couldn't sleep, I used alcohol to extract the energy from my body. Two months after returning to Selah,

I was completely addicted to alcohol and Marlboro cigarettes and yet, I worked and went to school and even started to excel a little. I bought clothes from the mall whenever I could and made friends with Courtney, my co-worker from my new job at another hotel in town. I sent half of my money home to Ammi, and the other half went to Deborah for living in her home.

Deborah finally bought the car of her dreams and gave me the Chrysler Sebring. She treated her Cadillac CTS as if it were made of her own body parts, cleaning it twice a day. The Chrysler became a ball and chain for me, because now I had a hundred-dollar-a-month insurance bill and a car payment. In addition, if I stepped out of line, I was threatened with the prospect of losing the car. I kept the peace in the house by obeying every rule Deborah, the Queen of Selah, made up for me. When she couldn't stand ordering me around every single day, her friend gave her the brilliant idea of creating a weekly schedule of chores for me.

I especially loved mowing the lawn with the broken mower. "A person who can drive a car really good, can mow lawns really good, so cut in straight lines. Make it neat," she said. It was a two-hundred-pound mower with wheels that barely worked, so I had to push it like a mule to get up the hill at the back of her yard.

Here was my schedule: Monday: clean the cat litter, replace with new litter. Tuesday: do laundry, fold towels exactly as discussed. Wednesday: clean house, dust, and vacuum everything. Thursday: clean the yard. Friday: clean the kitchen floor thoroughly and mow the lawn.

One of Deborah's friends was a pharmacist, and when I heard how much money she made, I decided that's what I wanted to be. I started taking chemistry and biology classes. I didn't pass any of them with good grades, because by then, my anxiety about Deborah's and everyone's needs was at all-time high. On top of school, I had round-the-clock work at home and my job at the hotel as front-desk agent. It all overwhelmed me. However, the more I kept myself busy, the more my mind recovered. I even started feeling as if I were a normal person every now and then.

Courtney finally convinced me to "give guys who like you the time of day." If she had known everything about my life, she probably would not have suggested that. I started to take her advice. Most of the men I met lost interest when I told them I was Muslim and would not be able to go out on dates. The few others who pursued me even after I told them I was Muslim were in it for sex, and two of them became my partners in bed.

At first I thought having sex with them was a good way to let go of my bad memories about human contact, but instead, it turned into a circus. Imagine going home to your own father begging you for sex with him after you had just had sex with someone else. It was downright disgraceful!

The men I had sex with did not have to be anyone special. I did not value my body back then. I could have been a prostitute. It was easy giving myself away. The two who succeeded just asked nicely, that's all. Their names are not even worth mentioning. I lay there and never showed any real interest, thinking, "Just please get off me so I can go use my rabbit."

I was numb. What made it worse was that when they tried to perform oral sex, my mind recalled how good it had felt as a child. I hated myself and asked them to please stop. One of the guys I messed around with talked about the beauty of my olive-colored skin and long, black hair. He said he wanted to marry me, but later he told me he couldn't leave his wife for me. So I went back to the relationship with Deborah's collection of vibrators. No problems there.

Courtney also went to the college I attended. She was a pretty blonde with big hips like mine and a black girl's buttocks. We ended up doing everything together, including sneaking away from school to shop two hours away in Portland, Oregon.

She became a good friend once I realized she did not want anything except my friendship. The only problem was going to her house where she, her father, mother, and brother lived harmoniously. I envied her. I had only dreamed of that kind of family. About the time Courtney became my true friend, we started going to the mall, which was our hang-out spot when school became too hard to deal with. She was very popular, since she'd grown up in town. She was well-liked by the few black men in town because of her shapely body. The entire Yakima Suns basketball team, who stayed at our hotel, wanted her badly.

One day in the fall of 2006, we visited the mall, hoping to spend the checks we'd made at work. We walked into Foot Locker, and there he was. I knew this guy could not be from my town; I would have seen him around. He reminded me of those guys I had seen on Black Entertainment Television back in Pakistan, when I had wished to find someone with so much confidence.

He had cool dark skin — like the Dark Almond Joy chocolate coconut bar I loved so much — and a shiny, bald head with cat-eyes beneath perfect eyebrows. As he walked toward me, I noticed his broad shoulders and thick lips that looked like the top of a freshly baked brownie.

"Hey, Courtney," he greeted. As he turned to look at what the kids behind him were doing, our eyes met.

"Who is this, Courtney?" he queried in disbelief. "I didn't know Yakima had pretty girls like this one."

He had a subtle smile — as if all were right with the world. A smooth reggae song played in my head, and I imagined a cool breeze from tropical palm trees blowing over me. This, in turn, made me feel a sudden calm I had never felt before. I smiled and walked nonchalantly towards the women's section.

"Oh, this is my friend, Laila. You've never seen her at the college?" Courtney asked.

"No way man!" he exclaimed. "If I had, I would've walked up to her and told her she looked like someone out of my dreams."

He then turned his complete attention to me.

"I'm Arthur Lavelle," he added in a smooth, melodic, Jamaican accent. He scrutinized every feature of my face.

"I'm Laila," I answered.

Courtney laughed — surprised has his reaction to me and continued to talk about school, while Arthur spoke about buying sneakers for his boy. I looked around quickly when he said that to see the offspring of this mysterious man. His son was six years old and even more handsome than his father, with curly brown hair and a lighter skin tone.

I turned around, and there Arthur was again, staring at me with the smile that made me imagine the cool breeze from palm trees blowing over my head.

When Courtney came strolling back to the women's section, she must have seen the look on my face because she quickly said, "I know, he's hot, right? He's married with kids."

I heard what she said, yet my feeling of disappointment quickly went away, and I could not stop thinking about him. Finally, I had come face to face with my perfect, ideal guy. I went to school the next day and took different routes than usual to my classes in hope of seeing him, but I never did. Days turned into weeks without my running into him.

I went on with my sometimes agonizing life for the next six months. Courtney was the only bright spot. About the fourth month, the sorcerer told me the embassy had notified him that my sister's visa was ready. I didn't know how to feel about it. I was not sure if I wanted Maya to come to the world I now lived in.

My sister had become my confidante that night when I told her the truth about our father. She'd held her tongue for years, waiting for him to make the mistake of filing for her visa. She couldn't wait to come to America. When he did what he did in Chicago, Maya cried with me on the phone, and when Deborah treated me like her personal slave, she said, "Just be patient for my sake, Laila. He will never send the visa if you leave." Once again, I had to swallow my pride and sacrifice myself. I adjusted my brain to believe I was in a war, and if I lost, my family would be left to suffer for years to come.

Maya's personality was sure to add fuel to the fire that already existed in Deborah's house. Deborah often walked around with no underwear, and while I lay on the bed, she leaned her crotch over my head and passed gas in my face. She took me to the Red Robin, her favorite restaurant, and in full view of the waiters, simulated fellatio by licking the top of the whipped cream from her strawberry milk shake. "Men love it when you can give good blow jobs," she said.

I became tired of using alcohol to cope. Instead, I used my money to spend more time on the phone with my family in Pakistan. Maya kept my secrets and my mother's sanity. She was now grown enough to have her own dreams. I told her about the guys who tried to talk to me and how beautiful they thought I was. She needed to hear that because she'd gone through the same mental abuse I had for having darker skin. According to most of our family, we two were "ugly ducklings." The thirty-year-old cousin with whom we had lived as children called to say,

"Even if you are pretty in America, you would still be ugly in Pakistan."

Maya knew about the zoo she was joining, but she still couldn't wait to set foot on American soil. She had to wait until the spring quarter was finished at the college before I could work for enough money to buy her ticket.

About a week before the quarter was over, I was upstairs in the school's two-story science and biology building. It was a sunny day, so before class I waited outside overlooking the courtyard. As I stood there watching students travel to their classes, I saw Arthur Lavelle again. Three girls walked with him.

According to Courtney, this was the norm for this guy. She talked about how smart he was, being on pace to graduate in a year and a quarter, which was two quarters earlier than the usual two years. By then, Courtney and I had already spent over two and a half years in school. When he looked up and saw me, he quickly told the other girls to go ahead without him. He hesitated for a minute and then gave me that smile I had dreamt of for months.

"It's really you!" he said from below in the courtyard. "I've been looking for you for months, but I never see you. Hello, Laila."

"You remembered my name," I exclaimed.

"I thought I would never see you again. I only see girls like you in New York or Jamaica," he answered, then asked where I was from.

"Pakistan," I said.

"Muslim?" he asked.

"Yes."

"So, are you looking forward to the summer vacation?" he asked.

"Yes, and you?" I answered.

He told me he was going back to New York and asked if I wanted to come along!

"No, I'm going home to Pakistan to see my mother," I said.

"Are you just saying that because you don't want to come with me to New York, or are you really going to Pakistan?" he teased.

"No, I'm really going to Pakistan to pick up my sister and spend time with my mother," I said.

"Do I even stand a chance with you, since you are Muslim?"

"Not really," I answered.

"Will I see you again?" he asked.

"Yes, I'll be back to school in September."

After standing in the courtyard for about five seconds with that sultry smile on his face — the one that made me feel at peace with the world — he walked away, vanishing underneath where I stood. I went into my classroom but thought about running downstairs in his direction, finding him, and telling him he did stand a chance with me. However, I kept remembering that Courtney told me he was married. I thought about him every day that summer, and I kicked myself for not exchanging numbers with Arthur Lavelle.

I sat in class that day wondering whether he really would have taken me to New York if I had said yes. I could not stop thinking about him until I reminded myself of how that other married guy had promised to marry me and then abandoned me.

I told Maya on the phone about seeing Arthur again. She chastised me for not giving him my phone number so I could talk to him over the summer.

I worked every day, sometimes eighteen hours nonstop, to buy the twelve-hundred-dollar tickets for my sister and me. I was not going back to Pakistan as I had before, broke and broken-minded. I had hope. I bought an Xbox for my brothers. For Maya, I had what she wanted most—make-up, and perfume, along with clothes I found shopping at the local mall where I had first seen Mr. New York. I bought my mother a brand new nebulizer for the asthma that was now overtaking her life, along with Dove shampoo, Pantene, and Tang. I also planned to pick up packets of the Bounty Candy that we had loved in Saudi Arabia.

At this time, Ammi couldn't do much without being out of breath. I knew what that was like, living with Deborah. My asthma and allergies made me a walking medicine cabinet. I kept my puffer, Advair, Zyrtec, Claritin, and Singulair in my handbag in full supply. I had gone to the allergist after feeling breathless several times.

I became extremely sick at Deborah's house. I often woke up with my eyes swollen from Brandy, the dog, sitting on my face while I slept. My health made no difference to Deborah. "My cats and dog are like my kids. I had them way before you came here, so I'm not going to get rid of them because of you."

The day of my departure came in June 2007. When Homeland Security went through my suitcases and handbags at the SeaTac airport, I was so proud when I saw all that I had bought for my family. I remembered the cherished days as a child when Aunty Salma came from Michigan with her family, bringing us Pantene shampoo and Dove soap for the first time.

I slept well on the plane, catching up on the sleep I had missed during months of homework, my hotel job, and gofer duties for Deborah and my father. The trip, which usually took a day and a half, felt like only twelve hours.

Except for the guy with halitosis sitting beside me on the plane to Dubai from London, everything went perfectly. The man tried talking to me several times, but when I did not answer, he got the message.

"You Muslim women—you're all the same" he scoffed. You think you're better than us," he continued, before turning away in disgust.

I arrived in Pakistan to find Ammi, Maya, and my brothers all waiting for me at the airport. They hugged and kissed me with tears in their eyes. After my year-and-a-half absence, they were fonder of me. I felt loved, and when we arrived home and everyone saw what I had brought for them, I felt respected.

My mother had created a feast for us, along with Aunty Seema and her daughter, Abeera. I ate that day until I felt euphoric from being so full. We sat and talked until around 1:00 A.M. about everything from Deborah's madness to how hard it was for my mother to deal with my father being married to another woman. I felt sorry for Abeera, the one who had accused her father of molesting her and ended up losing her mind. She sat there spaced out while the rest of us talked. I knew what that was like. I could easily have been her. Sometimes I actually had been her, especially in Mecca. Somehow, though, Allah had kept my mind sound enough to function normally. Abeera hadn't been so lucky; her mind was permanently broken.

The next day I felt a sick feeling when it came time to visit Uncle Asif, my mother's brother who had given me the hundred dollars before I left Pakistan the first time. When I was around ten years old, he had become deathly ill, losing his eyesight and looking as though Death had gotten a hold of his passport to life. A *malang* (priest) that Nani brought to his house told us he had been hijacked by evil. The *malang* looked selfless, but I didn't think he was capable of removing any bad spirits or spells. His white beard was long and shaggy, he wore dirty clothes, and he looked as though he'd gone hungry for days. However, people told us he was very close to Allah, as all he did was pray day and night.

He found my uncle's name written on the plaster wall behind his closet with some green or dark-brown stuff that smelled like filth when the *malang* burned it. Two weeks later, my uncle became well, even regaining his eyesight. He developed a big, dark mark on his forehead from weeks of praying and bowing for hours five times a day in thanks to Allah for saving him.

When I walked into his bedroom that day, however, I knew he was on his way to see Allah. He had cancer, and his wife said it was not getting better.

His liver was failing. She thought a jealous competitor had worked *kalajadoo* (witchcraft) on him again because his marble business was flourishing in Malaysia.

I touched his head, saying, "*Abu, Abu* (father, father)," and he lit up when he saw me.

"My daughter, I only prayed for the day I would see your lovely face again," he said softly.

When things became unbearable in my house as a child, I often went to Uncle Asif's home, where I was treated like his daughter. He was a loving man who required nothing for his love in return. He loved his wife so much that he worshipped the ground she walked on. They had renewed their vows a second time, throwing the equivalent of a big wedding in Pakistan. He became my true father after my father betrayed me.

Uncle Asif beckoned his wife to make a big pot of *paye* (cow feet) in curry, which he knew I loved. I felt pain in my heart knowing he was going to die. I could not eat at first, but when I saw him watching attentively, I swallowed as much as I could. Maya, Ammi, and I spent the day with him while my brothers went to school. That evening, I prayed earnestly, asking Allah to keep Uncle Asif alive and give him good health. My faith was nonexistent as I prayed. I knew he was going to die.

For the next couple of weeks, Mother, Maya, and I watched Indian movies with their typical love stories, choreographed dancing, and singing. Before that summer, those movies bored me because I thought they were so unreal, but now I could relate to the love-at-first-sight storylines. Standing on the balcony talking to Arthur Lavelle had made me feel as though I were one of those beautiful actresses being wooed by the lead actor.

My sister must have told everyone who lived in the Buffer Zone of Karachi that she was leaving for America. All her friends seemed happy for her, and they came to the house to wish her well. She had apparently become popular, being the most outspoken person they knew.

My younger brother, Jawad, was very happy about her departure. Pakistan had received independence from India on August 14, 1947, and he made it very clear he would get "independence from Maya" on September 14, when she and I left for the States. As I was packing my bags in the living room, he said, "You take Lazy Love with you, *Baji*, for my sake, please! I don't want her to come back, either."

Maya and Jawad's rift went way beyond sibling rivalry. She sometimes woke up smelling like the kerosene my mother used to make fire for cooking. Jawad stood over her with a match, warning that if she ever hit him again, he would light her on fire.

Jawad was a crazy boy! He also fooled Maya into drinking chicken's blood by saying it was pomegranate juice.

Several times, he tied the neighborhood children up on our roof, pretending to be a jail guard or a Taliban leader and beating them with whips made from small tree branches and belts. My mom hated the days she came home to the neighbors telling her to keep her evil son away from their children.

I left Karachi more worried about my mother than ever before. I had mixed feelings about my sister at times because she gave everyone in my family trouble. Although Maya could become nagging, she kept my mother from worrying about me and everything else while I was gone.

"I won't have anyone to talk to now," Ammi said the day we left.

Maya and I talked on the plane all the way to Seattle. Sometimes, I worried she would not approve of the crazy world I lived in there and just become another problem in my life. I had seen her defiance when my father tried to beat her when she was a child. She refused to cry and stared at him with such bravery in her eyes that he became scared and walked away.

Maya was not a passive person. She said disgusting and hateful things that killed the other person's spirit. My mother called her Lazy Love because she showed love to her family only when she wanted something from them. She was completely different from me. Nothing bothered her, and no one could make her cry. Maya was a ninety-pound rock who did not put up with anyone's insolence. How would she deal with psycho Deborah? I wondered.

Deborah and our father met us at the SeaTac airport, and Maya never even said hello. She was silent on the ride to Selah.

"Hey, Maya, how does it feel to be in the U.S.?" Deborah asked. My sister looked at Deborah as if she had asked her to strip naked. She said in her typical sarcastic voice, "It feels the same."

I knew then that this was going to be a battle to the end.

Chapter 18
Twenty-Three Years Old and Counting

School started for the fall quarter one week after I arrived back in Selah. My classes were chemistry, philosophy, calculus, ethics, and my sister Maya; she was in a class by herself. She followed me to school in the morning to get away from any gofer duties my father or Deborah tried to impose on her. She started smoking Marlboros as if she owned shares in the company and had received them as complimentary gifts. At home, she sat on the couch in the fetal position until my father yelled at her for not helping anyone in the house.

After a week, she fled to the bathroom whenever he or Deborah yelled at her, ignoring them both. One night at dinner, our father lost it and started to scream as loudly as he could. Maya walked away from the table and locked herself in the bathroom.

"If you don't come out, I am going to come in there and kill you!" he yelled, banging his head on the bathroom door as though possessed by the devil.

I came to her rescue from the kitchen, where I was cooking dinner for everyone.

"Stop the screaming!" I yelled.

He turned around, picked up the huge vase from the entertainment center, and threw it at me. I ducked and sought cover in the bathroom. My sister quickly opened the door before he could throw anything else at me. We sat there without eating dinner for about three hours, making sure he'd gone to bed before we came out.

Two days later, I was in the tutoring center seeking help for my failing chemistry class, and Arthur Lavelle walked in. Three girls and his friend Benny, who was half his size, were with him. I knew Benny from the school gym, where we worked out. As usual, Arthur wore clothes that I had never seen in Yakima, with a black, patent-leather Kenneth Cole book bag and shoes to match. His wore a white, leather jacket with lines of white stitching, which made it look luxurious. When he saw me, he stopped in full stride and deviated from his path toward the back of the room, where all the biology majors hung out.

"I'm really happy to see you again, Laila," he said with his signature smile. I don't know why I stood up, other than the fact that I was nervous and excited to see him. His presence was so intoxicating that I felt I had to get up to greet him. He hugged me with his huge, muscular hands and broad shoulders. For the first time in my life, I felt safe from harm.

"I thought about you all summer," he said, hugging me so closely I could feel his warm breath on my neck. Holding me by my arms, he looked into my face. "Did you bring your sister back from Pakistan?" he asked.

"Yes, she is at home." I said. The thirty people in the lab seemed to evaporate with every second he spent smiling at me.

"You know, you look like someone I've dreamt about for a long time," he said, holding my right hand with his left and unzipping his jacket with the other hand.

"You better take my number and call," he said. I smiled but did not answer, and he bent to write the number in my notebook. "Or you can find me in the dorms until the end of the quarter. If you need anything, Laila, just call or find me."

Arthur sounded so sincere that I felt he knew I had been in trouble all my life. After that conversation, I felt as though I knew him, although he still seemed very mysterious. He hugged me again and left me standing in a completely tranquil state. I slowly eased into the chair and knew that I couldn't do any work after that. I sprang up out the chair and grabbed the handbag I'd brought from Karachi. Leaving my books and coffee on the desk, I ran out of the room and dialed my sister.

"I saw him again, Maya, and he hugged me!" I said, speaking in Urdu in case anyone overheard me.

"He hugged you?!" she asked.

"Yeah, he hugged me, Maya. He is so big, I felt like a little girl hugging him. He gave me his number and said I should call." I was so happy, and she knew it.

"You should call or text him," she said.

"I will, right now." I hung up and loaded his number into the text box of my cell phone. I thought I wrote: "I was happy to see you, too." But I was so excited, I actually wrote: "I was see you, too."

I went back inside, quickly packed my belongings, and left the tutoring center. I had no business there. I was done for the day. As I walked towards the car, I saw Courtney. I ran to her and hugged her.

"I saw Arthur, your friend from the mall. He gave me his number, and I texted him." I said it so fast that I ran out of breath from running and speed-talking.

"You know he's married, right? And he has kids. I told you," she said, looking puzzled, as if to say, "Are you all there in your head? Are you hard of hearing?!"

"He said he lived in the dorms, so where's his wife?" I asked, searching for immediate answers to fix the confusion in my head.

"She goes to school right here at the college, and he has a son and a daughter. I've seen them both." Courtney said, viewing me with an uncompromising look. "Don't get caught up with married men," she warned. "Remember what happened to you with the other guy."

I'd never thought much about what had happened with that other man. The wounds he created were superficial compared to machete-sized ones the sorcerer had created over the years.

"Arthur's a player, Laila. He always has those girls hanging off him—and don't you have class now?"

I was slapped back down to reality as I turned around and walked to the class. Then I remembered the look on Arthur's face. I knew evil well, and it was nowhere to be found in him; my soul cried out that this man was a good man. I turned back around, walked to my car, and looked at my face in the mirror for the first time in a long while to see what Arthur Lavelle had seen that day. I saw beauty. I saw me. I smiled, started the car, and went to Deborah's house.

My sister sat on the steps, puffing away at a cigarette. I felt guilty as hell. I had bought her first cigarettes in Karachi after our father had introduced them to me. I sat with her, joining in the puffing, and told her what Courtney had said to me. I hardly smoked anymore, because when I ran on the treadmill at school I became short of breath. My alcohol addiction was still in full swing, though, to deal with new stress and old memories.

"You have to find out for yourself if he is married, Laila" Maya begged. "Call him now and ask him. If he says no, then no problem. But if he says yes, then stay away."

I agreed, but I knew calling him would cause butterflies in my stomach. "I will do it later when I have a couple of Smirnoff vodka shots in me," I said.

We went inside, where we made our favorite lunch: *palak ka-saag* (spinach cooked in butter and garlic). Or I should say *I* made lunch, and my sister sat and watched, as usual. She never did anything. She reminded me of our father. They both liked to be served like royalty. She talked to me through my chores, though. Maya was never lazy about yapping off. My phone buzzed as I put the spinach on the stove, and I saw the envelope signaling a text from Arthur.

It read, "I think you meant, 'I was happy to see you, too.' I know I am not Muslim, but I would convert tomorrow if I knew I had a chance with you."

I remembered telling him before I went to Pakistan that a non-Muslim had no chance with me. After consulting Maya, I texted back, "Well, in that case, the door is open."

He replied, "Then let me in."

My sister and I went crazy when we read that message. After that, I didn't care if he was married. Nevertheless, I liquored up and called him around eight that evening. Maya and I went to the car to prevent anyone from overhearing us.

"Hello, Laila, I've been waiting for you to call," he said.

"Well, here I am. What do you have to say to me?"

"Where are you? Are you ok?" he asked.

"I am home in Selah. I feel good."

He persisted. "You sound different. Are you all right?"

"Well, I had a few drinks. So?"

He asked the obvious: "Why do feel the need to drink on a Tuesday night?"

"I'll tell you some other time," I answered.

"Promise?" he said.

"Promise."

"I'm studying with Beth right now. I'll call you when I'm done, okay?" he said.

When he called back, Maya and I locked ourselves in the bathroom, where we pretended to bathe. She forced me to ask about his marital status.

"Are you married?" I asked.

"We'll talk about that in person," he said. "Why are you whispering?"

I told him who I lived with and said the current restrictions prevented me from talking freely.

"Okay. Meet me tomorrow, and we'll talk about everything you want to talk about," he said.

Later that evening, Deborah yelled my name about twenty minutes after she came in from work. "Laila, what is the meaning of this?" she asked, holding an overdraft letter from Wells Fargo Bank in one hand and the tub of cookie dough ice-cream she ate every night in the other.

She had signed me onto her bank account so I could cash my work checks and run errands, buying whatever she wanted, whenever she wanted it. I quickly sat up in the bed. The charge was five overdraft fees and a negative balance of $434. I knew the reason for the negative balance: With my sister around, I'd started buying more cigarettes, more alcohol, and more Mocha Braves from Starbucks.

"How are you going to pay for this?" Deborah screamed. "I trusted you, and this is what you did!"

I tried to explain that it was just an oversight on my part, but to no avail. She kept going on and on about how much she had trusted me not to betray her.

"I know betrayal," I insisted. "This is not betrayal."

Soon she and our father were by my bed, yelling at me. I thought about how much money they took from me to pay bills all the time and facilitate his trip back to Pakistan, which I never complained about. I did not say a word about this, but my sister spoke up in her deep Pakistani accent: "You people take her money all the time that she works hard for. What is the big problem now? She is you people's personal slave, so why the yelling about overspending?"

As she was talking, I wished I had enough money in my bag for a hotel, because I knew they were surely going to put us out on the street that night. They never did. Deborah yelled about disrespecting her in her own home and my father just walked away in disgust, saying to me, "You better take care of this. I don't care how."

I slept well that night, probably because I was drunk from the vodka, but anxiety riddled my body as I awoke the next morning.

"I have to get this money from somewhere," I thought as I brushed my teeth in the bathroom.

I called my manager at the Clarion Hotel, begging for extra hours. She gave them to me without any questions. I was worried. This money thing could become volatile at any time. I needed to take care of the bill as soon as possible. There was no way out.

Around 1:00 P.M. the next day, as I walked to the tutoring center to meet Arthur Lavelle, I thought about turning around, but my sister did not let me.

"He waits for you, Laila. Don't turn away," she whispered.

I was too worried about the money to meet or talk to anyone. But I walked in, and there he was, smiling and creating a calm mood in my mind again. We sat across from him. Huge books from microbiology, anatomy, physiology, and chemistry, along with a notebook, sat on the desk in front of him. He stared at me with a half smile for about a minute with one finger covering his mouth. "This is your sister? She's different but just as beautiful."

Maya smiled at me and started yapping off in Urdu to hide her feelings about him.

"He's a smooth talker, Laila. Wow, look at his shoulders!"

She then turned to him. "Thank you, Arthur."

He must have noticed I had not smiled back as Maya spoke. "What's wrong, Laila, and why were you drinking last night?" he asked.

As he spoke, I noticed his cell phone sitting on the table along with his car keys with the Acura sign on the remote. I looked at his face again, noticing a change in expression. Arthur's sincere look said, "Tell me everything; I won't judge you."

I had been good at keeping secrets all my life, but Arthur Lavelle had my number. I spilled my guts without even consulting my sister, as I normally would have done.

"I over-drafted my account, and my stepmother is so upset. I didn't mean to do it. It just happened, and now she is asking me for the money. I will have to work two weeks to pay that money off. I'm trying to pass my classes so I took fewer hours at work, but now I'll have to work forty hours this week."

"Forty hours of work and taking science classes here? Are you mad?" Arthur knitted his big, black, perfectly shaped eyebrows.

"I know," I answered. It's crazy, but I've been doing it since I came to this school."

"How much is the overdraft?" he asked, quickly changing his demeanor and putting his hand on the table as if saying, "Now it's time for business."

"A lot ... I'd rather not say," I replied, feeling so embarrassed.

Before I finished my sentence, Maya blurted out, "Four-hundred-thirty-four dollars."

I glared at her harshly, and she stared back at me as if to say, "What? What did I do?"

"Don't worry, Laila," he said. "It's nothing to be ashamed of. Right, Maya?"

Arthur picked up his Kenneth Cole briefcase from the ground, reached in, and took out a stash of cash. He counted out four crisp hundred-dollar bills and pulled another fifty dollars from another pocket of the bag. He put the money in his microbiology book and slid it toward me gently.

"If you ever need anything, Laila, never be afraid to ask me. And don't worry about working to pay me back. My mother always said, 'Ask, and it shall be given unto you.' Just focus on your studies, okay?" he added.

At first I hesitated to take his money, but then I thought about my sister and my failing grades.

"I don't lend money to people, so don't try to pay me back," he said.

"I'll pay you back. I promise," I said.

"No worry yourself, mon," he said in a thick Jamaican accent I had not detected before. "Everything is everything. Just study. School and work no mix."

I had heard a Jamaican accent before, back in Chicago, from a lady who bought Lotto tickets at the store where I worked. Arthur's words were like a melodic song. I yearned to hear him speak like that as much as I had yearned for alcohol before. We talked for about half an hour until it was time for my chemistry class. I opened up more that day after I realized things were not getting better at Deborah's house.

"Tomorrow you and your sister meet me for lunch," he said. I rose and started to walk away. "No hug for me?" he asked.

I wanted to jump over the table and kiss him, but I restrained myself. Instead I walked slowly to his side of the table and hugged him. He held me tighter than he had the first time.

"Come, Maya, give me one, too," he said, after he let me go. She looked so happy, she ran to him like he was *Shahrukh Khan*, her favorite Bollywood actor. Her feet lifted off the ground as he hugged her.

"Take care of your sister for me, Maya," he said, as he put her down on the ground.

I walked out of the building, grateful to Allah for providing Arthur. He reminded me how I felt when Nida saved me from myself back in Pakistan. I heard later that she had come to the school looking for my sister in order to find me. Maya gave her my number in the U.S., but she never called. I realized I hadn't told Arthur thanks for what he had done. I had never thanked Nida, either, and that had always weighed heavily on my mind. I quickly texted Arthur to let him know how I felt.

"I really appreciate what you did today. I will pay you back, and I won't forget it. Thank you so much." He didn't reply.

That afternoon, I deposited the money Arthur gave me. The balance now read sixteen dollars. I proudly placed the balance slip strategically where Deborah left all her gofer notes for me. When she walked in that evening and immediately started to complain about her mortgage coming directly from that overdrawn account, I directed her attention to the fridge door.

"How did you get this money?" she demanded, looking surprised and yet disappointed. The altar she preached from was closed.

I spun my head as she spoke and looked at her in disgust. Today she wouldn't be putting me down on the phone or in my face. "I fixed the problem. That's all that matters," I said. Deborah was obsessive about every move Maya and I made.

I went to the bathroom to prevent the grueling inquisition Deborah geared up to unleash. I imagined she would also say, "I'm just so nice. I help you third-world people to get visas, stay in my house, and get cars—for nothing in return. I'm such a good person."

She asked my sister about the money. Maya refused to answer. Minutes later, Maya joined me in the bathroom. We talked in Urdu about how much we hated being in the house with Deborah and her animals. The latter term, of course, included her husband.

By then, my father's entire obsession was about whom I was having sex with. After coming back from Pakistan with my guard dog, Maya, everything was off limits for him, although I did not really care what happened. That man became increasingly agitated at my sister for never leaving my side. If I was awake, she was up; if I was asleep, she was still up. She was on her regular four-hour-a-night sleeping schedule, but she went into the bathroom and jumped out the window to smoke a cigarette at three in the morning, which made her even more awake, so she hardly slept.

One night as I slept, I felt my father tugging on my hand. I awoke and followed him to the kitchen. "What is the matter?" he asked. He moved his head downward, which signaled you-know-what. I looked at the floor as the memories of how badly I had wanted to kiss Arthur Lavelle yesterday came rushing in.

I could not be with my father. It was as if I had gained back the little human instinct I had left after he turned me into an animal that night in Chicago.

I walked away, leaving him standing there just as I had done to Farooq, the Pakistani biker boy, because he looked like my father.

I went back to bed. It was the time of night the devil visited me in person, and my memories took over, sending me spiraling into depression.

Back in Mecca when I was ten, my father always sent my mother ahead when we went to any functions at the mosque. "We will catch up," he told her. I sat on the bunk bed—which had been divided for fear it would break and fall on my sister on the lower level. I would be fully dressed in my burqa, covered from head to toe, and he sat in front of me and begged. "Please, *Baji*, just one kiss. I am under a lot of stress. Help me out please, please, *Baji*."

I sat there and cried while he reached under my clothes as he kissed me, hurting me as he stuffed his fingers into my crotch. By the time he was done with me, I could not attend the function. I ripped off the scarf that covered my head and face except for my eyes, took off my *qameez* (blouse) and *shalwar* (pants), and then headed into the shower for a cleansing with scalding hot water. I don't know how I felt after those showers, but I remember my life in Saudi Arabia: I walked among the living like a spirit searching for its last resting place. I was a shadow of my prior self.

I specifically remembered those days that brought me severe pain. They occurred mostly on Fridays before 12:00 AM. Shoes were not allowed inside the mosque. Twice, I burned my feet severely coming out, forgetting to wear my slippers on the scorching, 130-degree, white tiles that covered miles around the mosque for people who had no space inside to pray. My mother asked me if I had left my head back home. Blisters did little to pull me out of the depths of hell that my spirit wandered into when I had no answer from Allah.

That night, as I stared at the ceiling recalling those prior days, Maya hugged me, resting half her body on me with her leg covering mine. Back in Pakistan before my brothers were born, she used to beckon me to get up and start breakfast. I had felt as if I were her mother back then.

I was in for a bad day.

Those mornings when I recalled my past like this, I would not bathe, brush my teeth, or even change the clothes I had slept in. I just boiled my two tea bags until the water turned black, made my tea, and went to school. I never spoke to anyone on those bad days.

Maya watched that day as I dragged myself around the house minutes after my usual departure time. She knew I was having one of those mornings and did what she did best: adjust. She glared and me and started to yell, "Stop this spinning around. Get going!"

By 10 AM, she had a bag packed for me with a recovery kit consisting of a fresh outfit, toothbrush, deodorant, and make up. She knew that when I finally woke up from my trance-like state and realized I looked disheveled, I would do my Superwoman impression, cleaning up in the car and coming back out with my pretend-to-be-happy face.

After learning nothing in my chemistry class — I left stupid most of the time. I walked out, slowly heading towards the spot in the back of the building where I could smoke and drink coffee just to feel a little better. I never made it. I turned around quickly and walked to my sister in the computer lab at the front of the building. She had my Superwoman kit ready to go. Seeing the look on my face, she sprang into action.

"Laila, you can't let Arthur Lavelle see you like this. Come, let's go to the car." We usually puffed on cigarettes before we started the transformation. We did it that way so my clean clothes wouldn't reek of tobacco and whatever else was in those Marlboro Lights. I quickly changed while Maya passed my deodorant and then my makeup. I drove to the coffee stand about five hundred feet from the main road to school. I swear there were more coffee shops in that town than good places to eat. I've yet to see that anyplace else.

We sat in the car waiting for Mr. Lavelle to call, hoping and praying for my upward mood swing to come. Maya was more excited than I was. I felt uncomfortable and started to count in my mind, "Sixty-five, sixty-six, sixty-seven…You whore… Sixty-eight, sixty-nine, seventy…You screwed your father and liked it…Whore!…Seventy-one…You were jealous of your own mother, you daughter of the devil!…Seventy-two…seventy three cars whizzed by.

Sometimes when the cars came too slowly, I counted tires, and then the gaps in the rims. When the big trucks came, I really became excited. My second brain took over.

Stop, please. Please stop counting! I begged my brain. Begging never worked. I reached in the back seat on the ground where the Smirnoff bottle sat from the day before.

"Come on, Laila!" Maya pleaded. "*Ya Allah madad* (Oh, God, help). It's 11:30 in the morning! *Patha nahi kya masla ha* (What the hell is the problem?). You get drunk all the time now, so *kis se baat karoon phir* (who do I talk to)?"

Maya had gotten my attention. I looked in the rearview mirror to see if anyone was watching and threw the bottle into the parking lot.

I quickly picked up my toothbrush and brushed my teeth right there in the car. As I did so, I saw him.

Arthur Lavelle pulled up beside my car in one of the nicest Acura trucks I'd ever seen, especially for a student. I knew, because I counted them. Nighthawk black, black leather interior, music blasting the rapper Kanye West's "Welcome to the Good Life," with the sunroof open, shining the sunlight on his face.

"*Ya Allah*, I can't believe he found me like this," I thought. I quickly threw the toothbrush between the seats. He jumped out, walked around, and leaned over my window. I smelled his strong scent, which smelled like the delicious cocoa tea I made back in Pakistan. I found out later it was the smell of Palmer's Cocoa Butter lotion.

"My Queen Laila and little princess Maya, good morning," he said.

I looked up at him, putting my hand over my eyes to avoid the sun.

"Good Morning Arthur," I said.

My sister waved at him, smiling.

"Let's go, shall we?"

As he opened the door for me, I noticed the children's car seat in the back of the Acura. He hadn't turned the music down. It scrambled any thoughts I had in my head. I was free. No counting. No recall, nothing but the knock of the bass shaking my body:

Welcome to the good life
Where niggaz that sell D's
Won't even get pulled over in they new V
The good life, let's go on a livin' spree
Shit, they say the best things in life are free
The good life, it feel like Atlanta
It feel like L.A., it feel like Miami
It feel like N.Y., summertime Chi, ahh
Now throw your hands up in the sky

We pulled up at the Chinese buffet called Floating Lotus, where I thought to myself, Wait, something is not right here. How is a student getting all this money? My mind formulated question after question to ask Arthur Lavelle. He didn't sit where the greeter showed him; he just went right to the buffet. I figured him for around 240 pounds, muscular, with a slight gut showing behind the cream-and-black Pelle Pelle sweater he wore. I realized then how he'd become that big. He quickly scooped up three plates of food, taking at least nine different selections from the buffet. This boy loved his food, just as I did. I picked up two plates and loaded each one with six different selections. Maya took one plate.

"I don't drink soda. Do you have any juice?" he asked the waitress back at the table. "Variety is the spice of life. You feel me?" Arthur said, as he dipped into the food on his plate. It was as though he were home eating dinner with his family. I followed, and I didn't feel ashamed to eat, as I always did in front of my family. When we were done, he beckoned the waitress to come over and clear the table, giving her a twenty-dollar tip.

"Twenty dollars for a tip?! I want to be that waitress," Maya said. We all laughed.

Arthur spread his hands out on the table and started talking. "Let's get down to business. I know you can't date because of your culture, so I'll make my intentions clear. I feel we are connected and will be together. I feel that way in my soul. For years, I dreamt of you but couldn't find you. I should've waited, but I didn't, and now I'm in a bad marriage. No problem. You're here now, and I know what I want. So, if you decide to be with me, you will be very happy with me."

I remained speechless for at least a minute, trying to digest the words I was hearing. Maya kicked my leg under the table. I spoke. "You said ... Did you say you dreamt about me?" I studied his face, thinking, there'd better be a good answer, or else I was going to think he was crazy.

"I used to see you in my dreams from when I was a teenager," he answered. "I saw your eyes and long, black hair. You were always trying to tell me something, but I was never able to hear you. Still, I could feel how you felt."

"Do you know how I feel right now?" I asked, looking at Maya to see if she was listening to Arthur's shocking tale.

"Yes," he answered. "I think you're happy, right here, right now, but you have secrets that you can't talk about, so deep down you never feel right."

He switched back and forth from his native melodic accent to proper European English, reading my mind as he held my hand. I felt connected to him. I felt he knew my every thought. I tried forcing myself not to think, afraid he would see the demons living in my brain, but that didn't work. He saw them. Question after question reaffirmed that he did see beyond the please-be-happy face where I usually hid my demons.

Arthur looked through me, not at me, and never lost eye contact as we sat there. "You can make your own choice, Laila. You're not a child anymore." He paused and then continued, "My mother used to tell me that 'if your right hand offends you, cut it off.'"

I felt compelled to tell him my situation. "My father is leaving the country to live back in Pakistan next month after Christmas, and I can't live with my stepmother. She is crazy and thinks I'm her slave."

Before I could finish, my sister chimed in. "She swears we are slaves she brought from Pakistan to take care of her. I can't stand what she does to my sister." She must have practiced that line at home because it was the best English I had ever heard her speak.

"I definitely understand your situation, and I appreciate you sharing this with me," Arthur said. "I am right now living in the dorms because my wife felt she owned me after our wedding day. I am a proud Jamaican man; I can't stoop to that level. So, no plans to go back."

"Are you getting a divorce?"

"What about your children?" Maya asked.

Arthur smiled at both of us, took a deep breath and started to talk.

"Well, it was very tough for them to see me leave, but in the end, some of the things that started to happen were just too much. Her mother once called the cops and told them her daughter might be dead. The cops showed up at my house, guns drawn. Now, you don't see many black people 'round here, so when you call the cops on a black man in a white neighborhood such as this one, anything can happen."

I understood what he meant, as Deborah had made it very clear how some people around town felt about blacks. I felt his pain when he talked. He was hurt but hid it well, or maybe I made him happy, which is what he told me later.

"What do you plan to do? You need to leave that house. You are not happy there," he said.

I wondered to myself, since he feels me, does he feel I can't afford to be on my own? I couldn't even get student loans because my so-called parents made too much money, according to Deborah. But with Deborah's lattes, ice-cream, Barbie obsession, vibrators, shopping sprees for decorative goods that ended up stored everywhere because she didn't need them in the first place, I was left alone, working to pay my college tuition.

It was as if I were thinking out loud.

"Come live with me," Arthur said with his everything- copasetic look and the subtle smile that soothed my soul. "We'll find a nice spot together," he said,

"Can I come too?" Maya asked, sounding as she had when she was little and wanted me to take her to the market with me. I looked at him quickly to see if there was any change in expression.

"I guess we can adopt her as our daughter because she's so cute!" Arthur Lavelle said, smiling with excitement at the same time.

We all had a good laugh, one that made the weight of the world disappear for the rest of the day.

Arthur decided we would lease a new apartment at the New Year, after my father left for Pakistan, to avoid any run-ins. This guy was no joke. He was so confident that I just knew I would not suffer anymore. His strength made me feel I could conquer the world. My sister and I said yes to all the plans and no to whether we were too afraid to take the risk.

As we left the restaurant, the waitress smiled and waved goodbye. She must have told everyone about her tip, because we were treated like royalty whenever we returned. In the parking lot, I first noticed the New York license plates on his Acura. Lady Liberty stood in the middle of the letters and numbers. As I walked to the car with my sister in tow, he grabbed my hand and kissed me.

After his lips left mine, he said, "I'm sorry, I've wanted to do that since that day I saw you on the balcony." I cherish that moment to this day. I was pure, and for that one moment in my adult life, I felt cleansed of my sins.

"I'm tired from eating all that food. Can you drive, babe?" he asked, handing me the keys. I wanted to feel this luxurious and shiny machine and eagerly hopped up to the driver's seat. He reached over, putting his head in my bosom, and adjusted the seat.

Maya quickly made her request before the music started blaring. "Do you have 50 Cent?"

"Yes, I do," Arthur said, reaching in his pocket and pulling out two quarters. Maya laughed. He got out the new 50 Cent album, *Massacre*. "Here, you can have it," he said, loading the CD in the player.

Ayo Technology came on. It felt so good to hear the music pump out of those speakers.

"This beat is sick, my man *Timbaland*!" he yelled over the music, smiling from ear to ear. I was extremely happy. I had dreamt of a moment like this when I watched MTV back in Pakistan.

I drove off, trying to pay attention to my direction with Arthur Lavelle bobbing his head to the beat. As we merged into traffic, he turned down the music.

"I remember where I was when I heard the first *Timbaland* beat. I was in Brooklyn, trying to find the house of this girl I had met at a party the night before. I could not believe what I was hearing. It was Aliyah singing, but the beat had a baby cooing in the background. This motherfucker is ridiculous."

I saw true happiness whenever Arthur talked about the music he grew up with. He was hip-hop, R&B and a little Coldplay, along with a sprinkle of reggae. Music made all his problems disappear, and adding me into the picture made life seem as though the greatest album he'd ever heard was playing constantly in his head. He later told me how he became dependent on music after his mother left him in Jamaica for the United States when he was nine.

Maya sat in the middle of the back seat, holding onto the rear of our seats and bobbing her head with

Arthur Lavelle. She was enjoying the music just as much. When "Candy Shop" came on, she danced in her seat, slinging her head from side to side, moving sexy, and closing her eyes as if she were dancing for some random guy in a strip club. To Maya, this was as good as popping in the 50 Cent CD, listening to "Candy Shop" on the floor of the bathroom, and masturbating to 50 Cent's voice. *"I'll take you to the candy shop, I'll let you lick the lollipop."* She loved that!

We believed in Allah, but everything we had been through in our lives made us do whatever we wanted, with no fear of retaliation. The skies hadn't opened up to rain down fire on my father, so what would Allah do about girls just trying to swim through their sea of sadness listening to hip-hop?

Arthur brought us back to my car in the school parking lot. Just as we arrived, my cell phone rang. There were seven missed calls on the screen, all from our father. "Where are you? Why are you not answering?" he demanded. Scared he could be sitting in the parking lot spying on me, I gave the phone to Maya.

"We're coming home now," she said after a long pause.

In less than thirty seconds, I went from feeling free as a bird to feeling like a caged monkey. I sat in my seat for about a minute, scared to take the phone back from Maya and fearing the barrage of nasty language and yelling I was about to hear. We arrived home after a panic-filled sprint on the small highway between Selah and Yakima.

"Call your mother," he said when I walked through the door. I relaxed as he walked out the door.

About six o'clock that evening, the phone rang. It was my mother, crying, and trying to talk at the same time. I feared the worst, thinking a crazy taxi driver had finally hit one of my brothers. "Your uncle died today," she said.

I threw the phone down, put my head in my hands, and bawled until there were no more tears left. When I couldn't cry anymore, I drank bottles of whatever I could find to get drunk on. Maya didn't cry at all. She just supervised me, fearing I would hurt myself being so drunk. Arthur called minutes after I finished a bottle of vodka. I felt compelled to answer, although I was in no shape to talk.

"Why are you crying, Laila? Stop and tell me what's wrong. If someone hurt you, they are as good as dead, you hear me?" he said in a tone that scared me. I told him my uncle died. Arthur became quiet and told me to come see him right away. I was intoxicated and didn't want him to see me like that, so I said I wouldn't go.

"Cancer can make you suffer harshly," he said. He told me about his cousin who had died at age thirty-five from Pancreatic Cancer.

"My uncle meant more to me than my own father," I said.

Arthur told me, "when things go wrong, something else must go right, so don't ever worry yourself."

I knew my uncle loved me, and he was going to have a talk with Allah, so something had to go right. I listened to Arthur Lavelle. I stopped crying and prayed for my uncle's soul.

The very next day, I went to Arthur's dorm room. When he greeted me in the hall, he locked himself out of the room, wearing only his boxers. I had fun with him holding me up and pushing me through the window to get into the room so I could unlock the door for him.

He had a big double room all to himself. Books sprawled over the two beds and both desks. I knew he slept with those books because there were some under the covers, too. As I opened the door to let him in, that subtle smile greeted me with such a warm invitation, I finally did what I wanted to do. I kissed him as he slowly walked forward in the room, pushing me backwards. He held me there saying, "You're okay now. I'm here. I wish I could have held you last night. I felt pain hearing you cry."

Tears filled my eyes as he spoke. I sat on the bed while he made himself comfortable, pulling books from under the sheets and placing them on the desk. The room was cold from the opened window at eight o'clock on a December morning, but I remained warm from the anxiety of seeing him. I welcomed the butterflies I felt that morning compared to the ones that had made me sick with nausea in the past.

"Tell me everything, and I know it's going to be hard, but you have to free yourself and let go," he said.

I did.

I released evil spirit after evil spirit as I told him every piece of my putrid past. Arthur Lavelle sat there with tears streaming down his face as I told him things I had never uttered to anyone before. I had told my sister the facts, but I had never told her how I really felt.

"I'm going to kill him. He is piece of shit that needs to be flushed down the toilet," Arthur said, after wiping his tears. He looked as serious as a judge passing sentence, and I knew he meant it.

I begged him for the sake of my brothers and mother not to do it. "He is not worth it, and you have a lot to live for," I told him.

We spent another two hours in his room until it was time for his biochemistry class. After he left, I wiggled into his bed with glee, putting one pillow between my legs, pretending it was him, and laying my head on other pillows that smelled like his cocoa butter body lotion. I fell asleep in a state of complete happiness for the first time in fifteen years.

Three hours later, Arthur Lavelle came back with my favorite foods. We ate spicy burritos from the taco store at one of his desks while I looked at his children's pictures. I felt torn. For the first time, I thought about being a mother and what it was like for his wife not having him around. I also thought how nice it would be if I had his child.

I wanted one of my own. His kids were beautiful, with cute eyes and curly hair. I became disheartened and irritated — I knew I had no chance of becoming a mother. There was no way I could bear a child for Arthur Lavelle. I envied their mother for being able to provide him with such precious-looking babies. I made a feeble attempt to forget about his kids, but I could not. My mind contorted into several different scenarios and feelings. Suddenly, I stood up, grabbed my bag, and walked out the door.

He came after me, calling my name and imploring me to slow down. "Laila, stop! Listen, there is nothing about your life you should be ashamed of. I'm not ashamed of my kids or my past. If you can't accept that, let me know now."

I only wished he knew it was not about him or his children. It was about my fears and my thinking I was worthless. I had told him so much already, but this was too much. I could not tell him why I was upset.

I was not even sure he would stay with me, knowing what he knew already, plus the loads of secrets I held in my corrupted mind, but then I saw it in his eyes. Arthur Lavelle was going to make me happy even if it took breaking his brain with the things that broke mine. He was sincere and selfless at the same time.

I held his hand and walked towards the hallway that led to his dorm room. I felt as precious as the gold bangles my mother hid in her bosom back in Pakistan. She had been holding onto them for twenty-seven years, waiting to see me married so she could pass her only earthy riches along to me. I knew Arthur Lavelle was for me, so I let go and started to trust.

I arrived home late that night. When I looked at Deborah's tracking device — my cell phone — I saw seventeen missed calls from her, eight from my father, and four from Maya. I called Maya and told her why I hadn't answered, but she didn't allow to me talk.

"They are waiting for you," she said. "They kept asking me where you were. They're saying you are out screwing everyone in Yakima. Deborah went into the bill and saw all your calls to Arthur Lavelle. They called him!"

I could hear the excitement in her voice. She was happy this was happening. Maya lived for those moments in which everything was in chaos. For her, it meant she was one step closer to ridding herself of her arch enemies. The fear was gone.

At home, I proudly entered the door, plopped myself down on the sofa, and saw Maya walking towards me, smiling. She knew what was about to happen. Deborah walked in with a printout of my forty text messages to Arthur, over fifty late-night phone calls to him, and another 112 texts to Maya.

"Who is your secret loverboy?" Deborah asked, throwing the bill at me. "How am I going to pay this bill when your father is sending all my money to your mother? Did you have fun? Because when your father comes home, he will deal with you." There she was with the Gestapo tactics she had used to scare me many a time before.

"The Selah police were looking for you," she added. "I reported my car stolen, and your father is going to put you back on the plane after the police take your visa. I'm your sponsor, and until you become a citizen, you are my responsibility. How dare you take my car to go tramp out in Yakima?!" she shouted.

I instantly became an insane person who didn't even recognize my actions, my thoughts, or my own voice! "You want me to come screw you! Bisexual! Is that why you called the cops on me? Because I don't let you go down on me? Nasty bitch! I was supposed to be your daughter. At least, that's what you said to me when I first came here. Mothers don't do that to their daughters!"

Maya sat on the arm of the sofa, like the devil in those commercials where someone is trying to decide whether to be good or bad. Coincidently, she even wore a little red dress that night. My words sent Deborah back to her purple bedroom faster than she had came out. She walked so fast that she hit wall instead of the door. Maya giggled while holding her mouth; she truly looked devilish that night. I heard Deborah talking to my father on the phone, telling him that when he came home, he must put me on the next plane back to Pakistan.

I thought to myself, This time around, that bullshit is not happening. Just the thought of Arthur Lavelle's big, muscular body made me as strong as he was. He had told me my rights as a resident alien and an adult in America. For the first time in my life, I perceived myself as an adult!

I walked into Deborah's room, yelling at the top of my voice.

"You can call your bitch, but he's not going to do a damn thing to me anymore" I yelled. "He knows that, and now you should, too. I'm going to move out on my own when I'm ready.

So you go get the bucket of cookie dough ice cream out of the fridge and shove it up your fat ass!"

I stormed out the room. Maya smiled ear to ear. We went through the door and lit up Marlboro cigarettes on the front porch. At the time, Deborah didn't even know we smoked. When my father came, he went directly to the bedroom without talking. Maya and I bathed, put on our clothes, and jumped into bed so that if he tried to throw us out, we wouldn't be half-naked on the street with our bags. He never came into our room.

The next morning, as I prepared for the hurricane to hit, I called Arthur, telling him of last night's events so he could give me some reinforcement. Somehow, he seemed to know what was happening before I even told him.

"If something happens, call," he said. "I'll come get you. Don't let them hit you, though." He was the smooth operator I needed in my life. Sade's song came streaming into my head:

> *No place for beginners or sensitive hearts*
> *When sentiment is left to chance*
> *No place to be ending but somewhere to start*
> *No need to ask*

He's a smooth operator …

Sure enough, Deborah and my father teamed up to scare me. The tag-team Nazis were coming, but I was ready.

"Why did you disrespect this lady in her house?" my father shouted. "You think you can come and go as you please and then disrespect my wife?"

For a moment, I was caught off guard by the "disrespect my wife" comment. I remembered the night he disrespected him after failing to answer her phone call while having a drink with a friend. He had thrown his passport and visa into the fire. Other times, when he begged me for sex, he cried at how Deborah grossed him out, insisting he had married her for us.

After about fifteen seconds I answered, "Your wife? Your wife!? You hypocrite! All this time you talk about her behind her back, and now she's your precious wife? Your life is a sham, Abdulla!"

"Is this true?" Deborah asked, aghast.

"Can't you see what she is doing?" he screamed, referring to me.

Maya and I hurried to the door as they argued with each other. We headed for Arthur's dorm. It was my new sanctuary.

I grew to love it there so much that he had to push me through the door when it was time to leave. I called my job, asking Courtney to cover me if they called, and we drove an hour to shop at the North Bend outlet. Maya was the DJ in the passenger seat, as Arthur slept in the back. After sleepless nights studying, his final quarter at the college was over, and he was now headed to Washington State University. He had also shown me an acceptance letter from Spokane's Gonzaga University with a scholarship. He was a nerd, but so smooth, it seemed he was three different people wrapped in one layer of skin. When we arrived at the outlet, it was like Christmas had come.

Arthur picked up whatever he wanted and begged us to do the same. I had never met a guy who loved to shop as much as Arthur did, and I'm talking about shopping for girls. He actually picked out jeans he thought would look good around the big hips my family hated so much. Arthur loved them, though, saying I was beautiful with "a perfect Coca Cola bottle shape."

We ended up with bags upon bags crowding the back of his Acura. As we drove back, Maya could not take the suspense anymore. She finally asked, "Are you rich, Arthur? Where are you getting these hundreds of U.S. dollars?"

He said nothing. He just smiled and looked at me as if I knew and it was our little secret. He avoided Maya, who turned around looking at him in the back seat. He seemed content spending in one hour what took a month for me to earn at work. As we headed through the hills near Ellensburg, Maya and I spoke in Urdu so Arthur wouldn't understand. I must have watched too many BET movies because I started to fear the worst about Arthur. I counted sixteen hundred dollars of his money spent in one week.

"I don't know, Maya, something is not right. He does not work and has hundreds of dollars all the time. You think he's a drug dealer?" I asked.

"Why he is spending all his money on us, I don't know." Maya looked worried, as if she were about to be kidnapped at any minute.

Chapter 19
Christmas with the Infamous Mr. Lavelle

On Christmas Eve, I woke up after three hours of sleep with an eerie feeling that something was going to go wrong. I dressed quickly to leave as soon as possible, trying to avoid any run-ins with the Gestapo. I was relieved when I made it to the car. I did not realize Deborah was now actively keeping track of the times I left for work. I was not scheduled to work until 1:00 P.M., so I went to Arthur Lavelle's dorm room that morning. It was a surprise for him; he was not there to receive it.

I called his phone three times before he answered. I wondered whether he had finally taken the offer of the voluptuous, pretty, blonde classmate who begged him to be with her. He had told me everything about her. Arthur had thought about being with her if I rejected him. When he finally answered, he told me he'd be there in three minutes.

I started to wonder where he could possibly be. If he was with his wife, who lived only a block from the dormitory, that wouldn't bother me much. After all, he was still married to her.

After three minutes and two seconds passed, it wasn't okay anymore! I was fuming with anger! How dare he try to be with me and still screw his wife! I thought.

Two minutes later: Maybe he's just spending time with his children because it's Christmas Eve.

Three minutes, four seconds later: He is probably with that blonde girl.

Just before my mind crashed with insane thoughts, he came strolling into the parking lot, smiling as he approached the car.

"I had to go spend time with the kids. Their mother told me they missed me and it was okay to come over," he said. I believed him. I don't know why, but I believed everything he said. I trusted him. We spent the morning together kissing, hugging, and filling our bellies with Taco Time Mexican food until I fell asleep in his arms. Arthur never woke me up; he said I "looked at peace sleeping." I awoke at 4:00 P.M., feeling tranquil, but then the phone rang. It was Courtney from work.

"Laila, where are you? You were supposed to be here at one o'clock. We called your house, and they said you weren't there. Are you with him?" she said.

"Yeah, Arthur didn't wake me up," I answered. I looked at the phone and saw nine missed calls: two from Courtney, another from Maya, and six from Deborah. I knew how to take care of the situation at work, but the so-called parent problem was beyond my reach. I quickly put on the white Kenneth Cole coat Arthur had bought for me, not sure what I was going to do. The phone buzzed, and a text message came in from Maya saying, "They are looking for you. Come and get me, please. They keep asking me where you are."

"How many times are you going to run away?" the next text message from my father read. Another came right after: "This time I'm going to send you back to Pakistan for good. If Maya starts to give me the same problem, I'll send her back, too. Deborah is already booking your flight on her credit card."

While he spoke, I recalled the time I ran away to the homeless shelter. I showed up there driving Deborah's car, bringing my three outfits and all my school books. I checked in, trying to get away from the madness. A man directed me to the office after seeing me cry my eyes out. I told the receptionist that my parents were being mentally abusive. She took my driver's license, told me the rules, and showed me my sleeping area.

There were six beds in the room, no bathroom, no windows, and it was very dirty. Most of the girls I saw there were addicted to methamphetamines. I recognized them by their rotted teeth. I could not stay there. After a couple of hours, I ran to the car, past the homeless sitting in front of the shelter with their cardboard signs.

After I snapped back from the flashback, I knew what I had to do. Once at home, I climbed in through the window and found Maya in the kitchen. We grabbed what we could carry in our hands, jumped in the car, and drove off. We headed straight to Arthur's dormitory, as we knew he couldn't wait to have us with him.

As I drove, I panicked, thinking the cops would get me before I made it to the dorm. I called to make sure he was there for me. "I've been waiting patiently for your phone call," he said. "Just park by my car, and I will meet you outside. Don't fret. You did the right thing. I'll be there before you get to the dorm." He was standing outside when I pulled up.

"Come, we have to get rid of this car before the police come to arrest you. That's what your parents would love to see happen."

We ditched the car at the back of the school and went to the dorm. As we moved our things to the room, Maya kept asking why I was crying. I couldn't answer because I didn't dare tell her the truth. Deborah and my father had traumatized me for so many years that I feared the worst. Arthur comforted me, assuring me the worst was behind me. We entered the dorm room and sat on one of the beds.

"You know I'll take care of you and Maya, Laila. I have something to tell you." He paused to wipe my tears. "I will never betray you; I am in love with you, Laila. You will be my queen as long as you treat me with respect and love me back."

Maya knelt in front of me on the bed. "We are going to be okay, Laila. Arthur will treat you right."

I stopped crying, flipped open my phone, and dialed my father's number. "The car is in the back of the parking lot behind my school," I said and hung up.

I had finally extricated myself from my jailers! Our phones rang and rang for ten minutes, until Maya and I turned them off permanently. Arthur bought us new ones the next day. Maya had started a job at

Macy's department store two weeks earlier and decided she wanted to continue working. She wasn't afraid of my father or Deborah, who went to Macy's several times begging and pleading that we come back. She just ignored them and continued to work.

I tried working the next day, although Arthur told me I shouldn't go to the hotel, fearing my father would try to kill me. I arrived just in time to watch Deborah leaving the parking lot. Within an hour, my father showed up twice, and then the witch came again, begging me to come home. I hid in the back office while my manager told them at the front desk that I did not want to see them. They kept calling and stalking me until I had no choice but to tell my boss I wasn't coming back.

Arthur was fine with that. He had commented several times that my grades were affected by too much work, so he welcomed my decision to quit my job. Maya, Arthur, and I spent Christmas day in his dorm room together. For Christmas dinner — Taco Time! It was the only place open in town, and I was very happy with that choice. We enjoyed every bit of that food and each other's company.

This was a sweet victory for Maya, since from the day she set foot in the U.S. she had made it her duty to get me out of the house of horror. From around six to ten in the morning, Arthur left to spend Christmas with his children. Maya and I woke up at eight and, wearing Arthur's buttoned-up Kenneth Cole shirts, we sneaked upstairs to the girls' dormitory to shower and brush our teeth. We had fun showering together and laughing about Arthur's loud snoring. It didn't bother us one bit; we really cherished him and everything about him.

That same morning around four A.M., before he visited his kids, I awoke to hear him talking on the phone to his mother for the first time. This became a ritual every morning.

Arthur's mother, Hyacinth, lived in Mount Vernon, New York. She called him first, forcing him to search for his Blackberry in our bed. When he found the phone, he and his mother talked about Creflo Dollar, the TV evangelist on Black Entertainment Television. They watched the show together and talked about the sermon for the day. They seemed so happy speaking to each other that I missed my mother and called her more often.

The way Arthur talked about his mother, we knew he loved her more than he loved himself. He told stories about how hard-working and strong she was and said she always supported him in whatever he chose to do. He said, "If it weren't for my mother, I would never have met you. She's the one who told me to be patient and finish school when I got fed up with my wife and wanted to return to New York."

Within two weeks, I knew more about Arthur's mother than about my own.

When he returned after visiting his children on Christmas day, he took our Christmas gifts out of his closet. For me, high-end perfume with an expensive handbag. For Maya, a white Kenneth Cole jacket to match mine. For himself, just what he wanted: me. The week we spent together in the dorm room became some of the best times of my life. Maya went to her job during the day, even though Deborah and our father still went to harass her there. She didn't care. In fact, she often dialed the phone and held it in her hand so I could hear what they were saying.

"You guys treated her like a child, like shit, like your personal slave, and now she left, so leave her alone," Maya told them.

One day they would say, "We love you guys and miss you," and then the next day, it would be, "I'm going to call immigration on you guys," or "We're going to call the police and tell them you stole from us. Then you'll become felons and get deported."

My sister was not moved. I worried a little, but Arthur was our personal lawyer who advised us of our rights as the threats came flooding in.

By the fourth day, Maya decided she wanted her belongings from Deborah's house. She just had to have them. They included gifts from her friends in

Pakistan and a cloth embroidered with the ninety-nine names of Allah that our mother had given her.

We couldn't just walk up to their house and demand our property. Deborah and my father were out for revenge, so we needed a different approach. Finally, Arthur stayed behind while we sat for two hours at the end of the block, waiting for Deborah and her bitch to leave. If Arthur had come along, it would have led to disaster if they caught us, so I begged him to stay behind.

Armed with cell phones in our hands just in case something went wrong, we parked Arthur's truck, jumped out, ran around the back, and jumped through the very window we had escaped from days before. My heart raced so much while we packed everything we owned that I thought I would pass out, but my sister was cool as a cucumber.

We packed up our stuff in black garbage bags as fast as possible, but as we put our shoes in the bags, the infidels came home. We laughed about it later, but when my father walked in, I literally urinated on myself! I thought the sorcerer would surely try to kill us and say they thought we were burglars.

My father had left several messages on our phones with details of how he would murder us if he found us. We ran into Deborah's bedroom, as that was the only door with a good lock on it. He had broken off the bathroom lock weeks before trying to get to

Maya. We dialed 9-1-1, as we had discussed with Arthur. Within minutes, the police arrived before the monster could break the door down. We jumped through the bedroom window and ran to the officer. I was scared out of my mind. According to Islam, if my father killed us for what we had done, his actions would be in the realm of a justified killing.

"What seems to be the problem here?" the officer asked.

"We are trying to leave, but my father won't let us. We are afraid he is going to do something to us," I said. Our father came rushing through the front door with Deborah behind him.

"Stop right there, sir," the cop said, putting his hand on his holster, "I'll be right with you."

I explained our predicament, scared that at any moment he would arrest us for being bad immigrants. I watched my father's eyes closely for any sudden moves.

"Sir, please step over here for a second," the officer said.

We walked right past him, grabbed our stuff, and loaded it into Arthur's Jeep. It was a proud moment for my sister, but for me, I wished the ground would open and swallow me up so I wouldn't have to look at my father and Deborah.

"Did you get everything?" the cop asked, standing between me and the infidel who had tormented me for fifteen years. I nodded as I looked at him in shame.

"Here is my card. Call if you need help retrieving anything else. If they bother you guys, give me a call."

We thanked the cop sincerely and drove off. The infidels stood there, helpless, as we disappeared in Arthur Lavelle's car.

On December 29, 2007, we were free from evil.

We spent the night partying in Seattle. We danced and drank the night away while Arthur stood guard. Maya became so intoxicated that she cried helplessly and paraded outside of the club, telling random people that we were free, that she felt good, and that Arthur was a saint for taking her along with us. It was her first time being drunk.

Arthur promised me that he would always take care of my sister. He walked by her side, closely watching to make sure she was okay. It was hilarious watching her, at five feet and ninety pounds, crying and acting crazy to total strangers, some of whom were thugs. It was the best night I ever had.

Arthur proposed to me the very next morning at breakfast at the House of Pancakes. I told him yes on two conditions, both of which he agreed to. He would have to become Muslim for the sake of my mother, and he would have to wait to get married until we could see my mother and get her blessings.

When I spoke to Ammi on the phone the day we escaped, she sounded so proud; it was as if she had broken free of the infidel herself. From that day on, she lived vicariously through me because I had done what she had wanted to do for a long time. Ammi only knew of the verbal abuse those infidels had perpetrated, but that was enough for her. She laughed, asking us to describe the look on our father's face when the cop came. Her years of suffering for me were over. "From the very first sign of abuse, I should have run," Ammi said, referring to the man who had stolen both of our lives.

From that day forward, the infidels became full-time, demonstrative stalkers, calling everyone on Deborah's tracking devices. She could no longer reach us on our original cell phones, but she had the monthly statements from them and called every single number they listed. People from my classes in school sometimes told me I was a bad person for calling the cops on my father.

The infidels finally sent an "undercover investigator" for us in the form of Saleem Bhai, the family friend who had paid my way to Pakistan the first time I visited home. Pretending to support what we had done, my father convinced my mother to find out our address and send Saleem to confirm we were living under decent conditions. Saleem listened to my mother, however, and never told my father or Deborah where we lived.

We arranged a meeting with Saleem around the third week of the year. He flew in from Chicago, where he lived. Deborah swore that Saleem was loyal to her and my father because he had borrowed money from them and still owed it, but Saleem had seen the verbal abuse firsthand, and he thought Deborah was a psychotic schizophrenic with obsessive-compulsive disorder.

He also saw how meticulous she was about all her worldly possessions and her disrespectful behavior to her husband, none of which made a devoted Muslim like Saleem Bhai happy. He was a simple man who believed in family and Allah. When he went back to their house after seeing us, the infidels demanded to see where we lived. Saleem drove around town aimlessly, pretending to be lost for hours until my father grew tired of searching for the "tan-yellow" house that didn't exist.

Saleem cared about us surviving financially more than anything else. We met him at the mall for lunch after he assured us whose side he was on. We worried, though, because he owed Deborah money. Arthur agreed we should be very careful. When we met Saleem by himself, we told him everything about Arthur Lavelle and our new life. He was happy we had escaped, but he cautioned us to become independent and stay in school.

Saleem turned out to be a better man than I expected him to be. He did not care that Arthur was not a born Pakistani Muslim. We left Saleem feeling secure that he could comfort my mother with the good news.

Ammi tried to act carefree on the phone, but I knew she worried for our safety. "Oh, oh, you're living better now. How are you getting money for all this?" were the first words out her mouth.

I knew then that everything was going to be okay. Saleem told my mother I had taken out school loans and would easily manage on my own. He told her exactly what she wanted to hear: We lived in a nice apartment with a professor from school who gave us a car to drive around town. Of course, I could not tell her the truth about Arthur immediately. My father had already tried to convince her I was with a black man. He told her I left because I wanted to screw the entire city of Yakima. Several times, my mother refused to answer the phone rather than listen to the blasphemy that man spoke about my sister and me.

I lied to my mother, refusing to tell her I was now living a life that was an abomination according to Islam. I justified the lies with the thought that the life I was living before was far worse. Of course, I was floored every time my mother told me what my father said about me. Sometimes I was a prostitute selling myself to the highest bidder around town, and other times, I was with a big black pimp who was selling me to whomever he wanted.

I cried when she told me about the phone calls she received from my elder cousins, aunts, uncles, friends, and anyone else my father found to listen to his self-righteous pleas for support. After fifteen years of destroying me physically, mentally, and emotionally, he now tried to destroy my character. He called everyone he knew in Pakistan, telling them that despite how well he'd treated us, we had called the police on the poor, sickly soul who was working to take care of us.

I held my tongue and didn't tell my mother the monstrosities that had taken place, sometimes only steps away from where she slept. Arthur implored me to tell her the truth about her so-called husband, but I could not. Maya told me it would send her to the madhouse, the hospital that housed the insane in Pakistan.

Chapter 20
New Year, New Life

On January 2, 2008, we moved into a two-bedroom apartment on the outskirts of Yakima. By the tenth of January, Arthur had started his new life studying nursing and psychology at Washington State University. I started school back at Yakima College. For the next ten days after school started, we spent close to ten thousand dollars furnishing our apartment. Arthur said, "Everything has to be in style when you live with a queen." Brown leather was everywhere, from the dining room to the bedroom. Two flat-screen televisions with subwoofers made every movie seem real. Maya continued to work at her job at Macys even after Arthur begged her to quit.

We finally found out how Arthur Lavelle acquired his money: gambling. He played blackjack with money his mother provided from her own stash and from the money he had saved with her from gambling. She promised she would continue if he stuck with school. She sent thousands of dollars via wire transfer when he needed it. Arthur told me how much money he had spent in his life, mostly from the gambling winnings. The first night we went into the Nob Hill Casino together, a small casino blocks from our house, he walked out with a thousand dollars in fifteen minutes.

I was in love, engaged, and getting what I wanted, whenever I wanted it. We made love for the first time on January third. Arthur told me, "The only way to forget bad memories is to make new ones to replace them," and, man, did he mean it. Arthur was a machine who never drank and never smoked. We made new memories of lovemaking that made me forget about my past. I still awoke from nightmares in the early morning, though. Arthur became my personal psychiatrist who prescribed healthy foods, no alcohol, no smoking, lots of lovemaking, and talking about every detail that had happened to me for fifteen years.

Around the end of January, for some reason, I listened to the voice messages my father left on the old phone Deborah had given me. I became paranoid that he would find us and kill us all. I wasn't too scared, though, since Arthur Lavelle was not someone you wanted to mess with. He was a nerd with so much information on every aspect of life that I felt I was talking to a walking encyclopedia, but he also had another side to him.

Arthur's other side grew up in the Back Bush area of Kingston, Jamaica, and was a rebel who vowed my father would see his last day on this earth if he tried to come near us. Some days I was okay with my father getting what he rightfully deserved if he came after us. Other days I feared it would actually happen and I would end up losing Arthur to prison.

During January, Maya, Arthur, and I lived the life I had always wanted. The demons that made me think about ending my life had finally been exorcized. However, a few feeble ones remained, causing random days of depression.

New devils popped up, too. We were home around February 2, when Arthur's wife showed up at our doorstep. She barged into the house after he cracked the front door to see what she wanted. She pushed her way into my bedroom, finding me in the closet where I was hiding, trying to put on my clothes.

"Where's that bitch?" she yelled. "You're the bitch who broke up my family! He is going to screw you over just like he did to me. I should beat the crap out of you," she continued. Arthur quickly ushered her out of the bedroom and softly told me everything would be okay.

"I'm going to tell your mother everything. You won't have a mother after today," she taunted him, storming down our front steps. I stood in the closet in shock until Arthur came for me. He assured me I had done nothing to hasten the end of his fledgling marriage. Arthur had his own demons, too. He had major trust issues. After I invited an old friend to lunch without telling him, he became possessive and checked my cell phone to see who I called. This made me very angry, as I had just left that kind of life behind.

Arthur's soon-to-be-ex-wife called his mother and told her that I had always been in the picture and was the real reason for their failed marriage. This, of course, was all a lie, but Hyacinth disowned him. His ex-wife also told his mother that I was Indian, and after Arthur corrected this by telling his mom I was a Pakistani Muslim, things became even worse for him. His mother, a devoted Christian, couldn't accept her son being with one of "the crazy people who blow up innocent people." Arthur began to distrust his ex after she lied to his mother. He had always considered her a friend and never thought she would betray him the way she had.

The phone calls and money from his mother — and the happiness these gave Arthur — stopped abruptly. He became a depressed and angry at the same time. He could not understand why his mother did not believe and stand by him. He started to spend less time at school and more time trying to keep up our expensive lifestyle.

Meanwhile, Maya became possessed by new demons that made her yearn for what I had. "I want a black man like Arthur; there are none in this town," she said.

Arthur tried to appease her in every way he could. He tried desperately to hook her up with Benny, his only black friend in town. It never worked. Though Benny was a good man, Maya wanted someone who was as extravagant in his behavior and as charming as Arthur. Benny was a very simple African a nerd with no "other side" like Arthur's. He was a good boy with a good heart, but he was not enough for Maya. Furthermore, Benny was in love with someone he couldn't have.

We partied in Seattle every weekend to keep her happy, but Maya hated Yakima and made it very clear she was already fed up with living there. The devil finds work for idle hands, and Maya had no school and no boyfriend.

Two days before my birthday, February 6, Maya's whining took a toll on me, causing me to lose my mind for that day. Arthur showed her just as much attention as he showed me, realizing that if my sister was not happy, I wouldn't be, either. Maya had him just as I did. They became really close. They were on same page, teaming up to deal with my bad days whenever I had nightmares about my father. At night while I slept, Arthur and Maya cuddled up and watched movies together.

Six-hundred-dollar weekends in Seattle, along with bills and shopping sprees, started to put cracks in the life raft we had used to escape. Arthur started to play blackjack at the local casinos until 1:00 A.M. to buy us whatever we wanted. He also sent money to his daughter, who lived in New York. She was fourteen. His daughter, Keisha was born out of wedlock when Arthur was twenty. That's how we found out how old Arthur was. We estimated it from how old he was when he had his first daughter. He had been 20 at the time, which made him 34.

Chapter 21
Run From Evil

I became increasingly unstable as my dreams became more frequent. I started to believe my father was a true *jadogar* (warlock). I knew he was capable of anything, and he was now in Pakistan actively trying to find someone to listen to him. My mother grew fearful that he would find a Muslim fundamentalist to come after us, as he had vowed the night he arrived in Pakistan. She feared for our lives, knowing the chaos he was capable of creating.

Arthur, on the other hand, waited with excitement for my father or his male friends to make the mistake of showing up. He had two, fully loaded, nine-millimeter pistols waiting for them.

From the day my father arrived in Karachi, he woke up every morning and tormented my mother, asking her to tell him where we were hiding. He went from house to house, telling everyone he had taken us to the U.S and we had repaid him by running away. When Ammi told me how sad and angry he was, I started to miss him! Imagine! Here I was with the man of my dreams right beside me, and I could not forget about that horrible man. My feelings were so inconsistent that I had no choice but to tell Arthur, hoping he would have an explanation for the madness.

"That's caused by years of him brainwashing you, Laila! He brainwashed you from a very young age, but time heals all wounds. A year from now, this won't be happening," he insisted.

How could I forget what my father was doing? My mother told me every word he said when he threatened to kill us or send our names to Muslim fundamentalists who would then do the job. Except for my mother and brothers, who never once turned against me, he now had my entire family behind him.

They thought we were just being rebellious, Americanized girls who didn't want to adhere to the rules of Islam anymore. Like Maya, I began to wonder if Yakima was the best place for us. When Arthur announced we were moving to New York before summer, we were utterly overjoyed.

Spring came quickly, and by then, I had unintentionally succeeded in bringing Arthur Lavelle down to my paltry level of academic success. We were both failing all our classes because we spent so much time with each other. We couldn't get enough. On top of the issues with the sorcerer, money became scarce. On April 7, we listed our precious items on craigslist and sold them all within three days.

Arthur Lavelle visited his local children and called his sister to arrange for our temporary lodging in her Connecticut home until we can find a place in New York. Maya grew ecstatic about living in New York. I did too. I had fallen in love with that city watching the *"Sex in the City"* series and the *Maid in Manhattan* movie.

We then packed bags upon bags of clothes accumulated from our constant shopping, put them all in the Jeep, and drove off, leaving Yakima in the middle of the day for the three-thousand-mile, forty-four-hour, two-day trip. The last thing we did? Downloaded six albums from iTunes for the trip and ate Taco Time tacos for the final time.

We left Yakima around 3:00 P.M., driving nonstop to Spokane with loud music blasting. Then we headed into Idaho and reached Montana around midnight. Arthur drove all night except when I relieved him for an hour or so around 4:00 A.M. He woke up, switched seats with me, and kept driving, stopping only for food. When we entered the winding hills of Route 80 in South Dakota, the snow came. The storm worsened rapidly, and within minutes we could only see a few feet in front of us. Arthur slowed the car down, lowered the music volume, and started talking about renting a room at the nearest hotel to avoid what we now realized was a blizzard.

Seconds later, Arthur turned the wheel to avoid a tanker and a police Chevrolet Suburban that had crashed together in the middle of the road. We braced for impact as the Jeep slid narrowly by the side of the gas-filled truck and slid deep into the ditch that parted the highway's eastbound and westbound traffic. Maya and I screamed. My sister, who never wore her seat belt, tumbled into the front with the bags that were stacked in the back seat.

I thought I was dead. I imagined that those demons were trying to kill me before I ever made it to New York. When the Jeep came to a halt three-quarters covered with snow, we looked at each other, scared out of our minds but happy to be alive. We knew we had no chance of getting out of the car or backing it out of the ditch. I watched uncomfortably while Arthur kept putting the car in 4-by-4 and reversing and forwarding. It was futile; we were in too deep. We worried that if the snow kept falling, we would be buried in snow by nightfall.

We also worried that other cars and trucks would slide off the road, hit us, and finish the job of killing us. Unlike other times when I had been ready to die, now I was petrified of losing my life. I had love and everything to live for. I became angry thinking about dying when my dreams and happiness had just started to come true. Finally, Arthur somehow pried his door open and barely made his way in the minus-ten wind-chill weather to the police Suburban. I watched, holding my breath while eighteen-wheel trucks slid and hydroplaned almost close enough to slam into us.

I worried as Arthur disappeared into the snow behind the car. Maya and I couldn't take it any longer. After he took what seemed like an eternity to come back, we jumped out, using Arthur's heavy school book covers to dig around the car tires. The treacherous conditions of the blizzard's wind and snow barely allowed us to keep our balance. Arthur finally came back, demanding we return to the warmth of the vehicle before we froze to death.

"It doesn't look good, guys. The cop is saying it will take at least till tomorrow to get us out of this ditch."

I felt cursed. Here I was again, stuck with no control over what was going to happen to me. My sister and I prayed to Allah that He might find it reasonable to help us. Three hours passed without help, and we were running out of the fuel that kept the Jeep warm. Finally, a tow truck showed up.

"Praise be unto Allah," Maya and I yelled.

We thought we were rescued, until the tow-truck man made it clear he was there only to tow the police car and the truck to clear the road. Arthur begged him to help us, but he only offered to take us a mile down the highway to the nearest hotel, leaving the Jeep there until the blizzard cleared. Arthur wouldn't hear of it. He knew that if we left the car there, we wouldn't have a car next day to go to New York. He ran back to the Jeep, grabbing the Kenneth Cole bag where he kept the money we made selling our belongings in Yakima.

"I have to bribe this motherfucker," he said, taking out two one-hundred-dollar bills. He ran back to the guy, who by now had moved the tractor-trailer out of the road.

Minutes later, Arthur showed up with the tow-truck operator, who hooked up a cable to the back of our Jeep and, slowly but surely, dragged it out of the ditch. We drove on, praising Allah for our good luck.

We spent the next ten hours in a hotel a mile from where we almost lost our lives. For the first time in two months, I needed a cigarette to calm my nerves. Arthur bought a pack for me, and for the first time, he joined us, puffing away at our Marlboro Lights outside the hotel room. We laughed as he choked on the smoke several times.

The next morning at around eleven, we continued our journey on the highway. As we drove, we saw at least thirty cars in the same ditch that had held us hostage the night before. By the time we arrived at the South Dakota border, it had stopped snowing, but it was still cold and windy. The wind caused the Jeep to swerve uncontrollably on the highway, sometimes throwing in towards cars in adjacent lanes. We were elated when the wind subsided. It seemed to take us forever to get out of harm's way.

We crossed into Wisconsin and drove two or three hours into Chicago, where I started having flashbacks from when my father and I lived there. I remembered how submissive I had become after his unsuccessful suicide attempt. Back then, I was a grown woman trapped by my mind and my loyalty to my family, but now I was free.

The next morning on our now-three-day trip, I became really ill. I thought it was stomach flu. At the border of Ohio and Pennsylvania, Arthur suggested I take a pregnancy test. He had noticed I was getting morning sickness frequently. I hung my head. I felt I could never become pregnant because of the sexual abuse my own flesh and blood had perpetrated on me when I was only a child. I started crying uncontrollably, unable to contain my emotions. Arthur quickly pulled over and told me never to feel ashamed or take responsibility for what had happened to me.

"It is not your fault. God is not going to take away your ability to have children after all you have been through." He was so convincing that I immediately became excited about the possibility of carrying his child. We finally stopped at a New Jersey convenience store, but I was too nervous to take the test until we arrived in New York.

At three o'clock on April 10, 2007, we drove over the George Washington Bridge, overlooking Manhattan and the Empire State building. We pulled up at Arthur's mother's house in Mount Vernon, where he had spent some of his childhood. She lived in a huge, hilltop house on a corner. At first, he went inside the gate and knocked on the front door, but she didn't answer. Then he went to the back, where the door was open. We went up the three flights of stairs that led to the attic apartment to find his niece in the kitchen, styling someone's hair. Arthur told us that was what she did for extra money. I felt nervous, as it was the first time I was meeting his family. She greeted us nonchalantly, saying just, "Hi," and nothing else. She did not seem happy to see us.

Arthur Lavelle had told me at least a hundred times about his niece. He felt as though she was his sister, since she was closer to his age than his real sister, to whom he referred as his second mother. She had taken the place of his real mother when she left him in Jamaica at age nine. I was shocked that his niece seemed so unhappy about our arrival and assumed that everyone was against Arthur being with me. We did not feel welcome one bit and soon realized that we were on our own.

My sister and I headed to the bathroom, where we spent a while trying to make ourselves look presentable after traveling so far. After applying make-up, brushing my teeth, and combing my hair, I pulled out the pregnancy test we had bought in New Jersey. I held it under my crotch and peed on it over the toilet. While I held it in my hand, Maya read the directions to understand the result. I thought about my mother and wondered how she would feel if I were pregnant. I thought about Arthur and how good he was to me, and of my sister who had helped me get out of that house of horrors.

Our lives were far from easy in New York for the next six months. Arthur worked at a posh private club in Purchase, New York, while we waited for him in the parking lot or went shopping. His mother had convinced his sister to renege on her promise to let us stay in her three-bedroom country home in Brookfield, Connecticut. Sometimes we looked for jobs during the day, feeling we had to help Arthur because I had caused him to lose his family.

Arthur told me differently, but I knew that if he had returned to New York by himself, he would not be sleeping in the parking lot. Several times we were tempted to blame him, as this was not the lifestyle we thought we would be living in New York. He worked hard until we moved into a one-bedroom apartment in Stamford, Connecticut, near the beach. Maya and I had found this beautiful neighborhood one day on our random routes to kill time. By June, Maya and I had also found jobs. I was a cashier, but the job made my feet hurt so badly I had to quit by early August. Arthur made it clear I would never have to do anything that made me uncomfortable.

Chapter 22
Time Heals All Wounds

My mother accepted Arthur when I told her about him, calling him her son and thanking him for rescuing her daughters. After months of therapy from Arthur, I finally told Ammi everything that had happened in my lifetime. I no longer blamed myself for any part of the fifteen years of despicable acts that snatched my childhood away. Ammi had not known her own husband could be so evil, and she blamed herself for not protecting me from him.

On July 4, I waited at home for Arthur to show up from the swanky golf club where he worked. Then we went to Sammy's, our favorite restaurant in a place called City Island in the Bronx, which was quite a treat for me. We drove to a strip of land surrounded by beaches where there were seafood restaurants of all types. At Sam's, we ordered Caribbean scampi and spicy red snapper.

For the first time since leaving Yakima, Maya was not with us. At the restaurant, Arthur started to tell me details of the conversations he had with my sister all those nights when they stayed up late watching television. I suddenly saw fear in his eyes and realized he was greatly concerned. He told me why Maya was not with us and why he didn't think she was going to be with us anymore. I immediately started to wonder if this was the right man for me. Was he about to betray me in some way?

"Maya loves you," he said, "but she wants someone for herself, and, furthermore, she wants a black man like me. She is tired of being the third wheel and has moved in with a man she hardly knows."

I was shocked, but I became apprehensive because I knew there was even more. He used the same tone of voice as when he once told me that he and Maya were drunk and had almost betrayed me. Arthur looked at me sternly and talked about another night when they had not been drunk. That time around, it was not about what Arthur had done with my sister, but what my father had done to her.

"She refuses to tell you, Laila," he said, "but I think some of the things that happened to you also happened to Maya. Whatever occurred, she has buried it so deep that she can't tell you.

"When she asked me why you didn't tell your mother about your father's abuse, I explained to her that the mental trauma you suffered was so drastic that it was not easy to tell anyone what happened."

"What did she tell you, Arthur?" I asked, growing furious with him for talking so slowly. I trembled, and my mouth became dry. I quickly summoned the waiter to pour more water for me.

"Apparently your father went home to Pakistan while you were in Yakima working and going to school."

"Yes, it was during Christmastime after I went back to Pakistan the second time," I said. Arthur continued to talk in a slow, calming voice.

"Maya said he woke her in the middle of the night. She went out to the living room with him to ask him what he wanted. He tried to take her clothes off, but she held her own. Instead, she asked him whether the only reason he wanted to do things with her was because you were gone. She asked him why all those years he had not tried to do things with her.

It sounded as if she were trying to reason out with him why it had been you and not her. He never answered her." Arthur continued to talk while cautiously watching to see if my mood was changing to a point at which I could not cope anymore.

"Maya said she told him he was not going to touch her as he had touched you, and she ran to her mother's room. She admitted only that he grabbed her breast, but I think more things happened to her, Laila. At first, I think Maya was traumatized into thinking she was not good enough for him to want to do the things he did to you. Then, when he visited Pakistan without you, she convinced him to get her a visa, thinking, as you had, that she would be stuck in Pakistan forever if she didn't do whatever he wanted."

I saw Arthur's concern. Throughout our lives, Maya had always wanted the same treatment as me, her older sister, so I accepted Arthur's theory and became furious at my father. I could not eat, and we wrapped up everything to go.

We talked for a while about what could have made Maya leave us abruptly, and whether it was caused by trauma and psychological damage by my father. We jumped into the Jeep and drove to Port Chester, New York, where Maya now worked. Arthur went into the store and called her out to the car, where we talked for an hour. We told her what we surmised and how she could fix the damage, but she didn't listen and said she was going to be okay. Maya had never stopped being a strong-willed person. It was time for her to find what made her happy, as I had done. For me, it was time to let go and live life for myself and my new family.

For the rest of the summer, Arthur worked hard to make my time in New York as pleasant as possible until it was time to attend school again. We were never short of drama in our lives, but we loved each other, so it was easy to let go of anything that bothered us. I enjoyed every day he came home to me, always looking forward to see what surprise he had in mind. Sometimes it was just a little thing like going to New York City to eat, but it meant the world to me. From my point of view, I was just happy to be permanently away from my father.

We moved to New Haven in September, two blocks from a school that would take all of our out-of-state college credits. We started school at a Connecticut State University without my sister around. We grew closer, as now it was only he and I. Unable to accumulate nice furniture, as we had in Yakima, we lived in a modest apartment.

On Thanksgiving Day, November 27, 2008, at 4:30 A.M., our son, Zain, was born at the Yale Hospital maternity ward with my sister and Arthur by my side.

"Time heals all wounds, but only babies can give you new life." Those are the words Arthur said minutes after our baby was born.

After I saw my son's perfect face for the first time, it did not take long to renew a real spiritual relationship with Allah. I maintain a close relationship with Him up to this day. I am still a Muslim, and so is my Arthur. He became Muslim to appease me; I don't think he really believes there is anyone in control of this insane world.

Somehow my putrid past disappeared when I realized I had a new life and family. Arthur has been right about everything so far, including the idea of my relinquishing self-blame for everything that happened in my past.

Once I did that, I was able to love myself more than ever before. I am strong, in control, unashamed, and no longer afraid of my past. I don't really think about the things that happened to me anymore. Instead, I live in the present and look forward to the future with my new family. The only numbers I count now are the 1-2-3 nursery rhymes with our son.

The Authors' Biography

Brian Arthur Levene was born in Kingston, Jamaica, on October 24, 1973. He grew up in Back Bush, one of Kingston's roughest urban ghettos. His mother taught kindergarten until leaving Jamaica in 1983 for the United States, leaving Brian and his older sister behind.

Two years later, Brian passed his sixth-grade exams and earned a place at Jamaica College, one of Kingston's top three high schools. In 1988, before he graduated, one of the most powerful hurricanes ever ripped through Jamaica, displacing hundreds of Kingston's citizens, including Brian. He reunited with his mother in Mount Vernon, New York, where she lived. In the States, Brian's interests shifted from academics to writing poetry and songs, producing music, and playing semi-professional golf.

In 2001, Brian moved to Palm Beach, Florida, to focus strictly on semi-professional golf, traveling to tournaments throughout the United States. In 2007, he relocated to Yakima, Washington, after deciding to pursue a career in the health field in order to benefit others. After receiving an associate's degree in science at Yakima College, he started school at Washington State University, in January 2008. He transferred to Southern Connecticut State University in August, where he studied public health. He started to write his first and second novels in his senior year.

Graduating in December 2010 with a bachelor's degree in public health, Brian published this first novel, *Not Easily Washed Away*, in April of 2011 while pursuing his master's degree in biology education at S.C.S.U. He now hold a Master's in Forensic Psychology and pursuing a Doctorate in Clinical Psychology.

Brian's co-author is his wife, whose pen-name is Anon Beauty and whose life inspired this book. They now live in Chicago with their two-year-old son, Zain.

The Book *Real Beast* is the follow up *Not Easily Washed Away* as Laila's life progressed with her husband and child.

Other Titles by the Author

Real Beast
The Terrorist's Daughter: T.O.G.G.L.E
Inconsiderate Bastard
Whitewashed Justice
Or visit
http://www.realbeast.org

Gully Gods Publishing

The Unique Multicultural Publisher

Anon Beauty & Brian Arthur Levene

Made in the USA
Middletown, DE
25 March 2021

36186748R00175